# A DOG'S LIFE

## ANN-MARIE WADE

ISBN-13: 978-1511552363
ISBN-10: 1511552360

# DEDICATION

*To Fella without whom we would not have learnt to be decent humans.*

# CONTENTS

# CHAPTER 1

## *Introduction*

The name's Bond. Fella Bond. Oh alright – it's Fella Wade (although my full civilian name is FellaBellaBubbaliciousBabyBoyWade). As I creep through the undergrowth, searching out the enemy, I sense danger ahead. It is only my bravery, alert senses and subtle stalking techniques that will allow me to catch my foe the dastardly – Oh no! What was that? A rabbit! I must get out of here as quickly as I can!

"Fella! Come on boy." Relief! She Who Must Be Obeyed is nearby and will save me.

"Ah, baby boy, did you get a fright, did you? Did you?" She wraps her arms around my neck like my warm blanket and I feel safe again. Why do rabbits scare me? They seem to gang up on me and jump out at the last minute when I least expect it. My heart is beginning to calm down as she tickles behind my ears and offers me a heart shaped biscuit. All is well again.

I should tell you something about my People. I will start with my official owner (for it is she whose name is on the Kennel Club Certificate and whose mobile number is etched onto my dog tag.) Her pedigree name is Wade. Ann-Marie Wade, but she is also 'She Who Must Be Obeyed'. She is also my Mummy. I love her and I know she really loves me. I have heard her say she loves me more than she loves her children. I expect it is true. It is not difficult to see why. Apparently it is because I do not answer back, am always pleased to see her and love her unconditionally. I am not sure about that last one as, of course there must always be conditions, don't you know. In fact these are tied up with why I am always pleased to see her because when I see her, I see food opportunities. It is she who feeds me my breakfast and tea and gives me little treats after walks and from her plate after her feeding time. As for not answering her back, it's simply because I can't. However, if she could hear my thoughts she might not think so highly of me. For example, at the weekend my People want a lie in – I am thinking evil thoughts, willing them to get up to feed and walk me. Usually if I stand on the first two stairs and sigh heavily she hears me. This is accelerated to a gentle whine if not and then a full throated bass tone bark if she is so far under from the previous night's alcohol that she cannot hear her Baby Boy.

He Who Must Be Obeyed is a little more complex. He is an Arsenal supporter and for that very reason alone he has assumed I would have the same allegiance. I do not. Nonetheless, as I begin this memoir, I have to wear an Arsenal collar and eat out of an Arsenal bowl. It does make it difficult to convince the two Tottenham supporting Rottweilers at number 22 that I really secretly support West Ham.

I have heard She Who Must Be Obeyed call He Who Must Be Obeyed 'wishy washy.' Apparently this is because he chops and changes his moods like the weather and I would have to agree with this. One minute he's got me on the floor and we are having a brilliant tug of war with my rope bone, then the next he's complaining about all the fur he has on his Abercrombie and Fitch T-shirt. One minute I am a 'gorgeous boy' the next I'm a 'hairy smelly mutt'. Cheek! And he has the nerve to act disgusted when I lick my Man Parts – we both know he's jealous!

No it is definitely Mummy who is the Alpha (fe) Male in our house. She is my Be All And End All. I am her Baby Boy. She has three daughters and a step daughter. I am her son.

Now for me – I am a stunningly handsome (and at the time of starting my memoirs) five year old black Labrador with a fine pedigree. I was born on 12 August 2004 and I am registered with the Kennel Club as 'Lyons Range Happy Harrison' and although I hail from Braintree Essex, I am from noble stock. My Birth Mother's name was Flakes Surprise and her parents were Lewis Pork Chop (slightly dodgy – they were the Essex branch of the family) and Sapphire Queen. My Birth Father's name was Lettermore Nugget and his parents were Tasco Broom Tip of Carnochway and Lettermore Quail Too (rather more distinguished). And that is what makes me posh. Hopefully, by now, you can hear my 'voice' – very well spoken, don't you know. It is of no surprise to me that my particular fortunes have brought me to grow up and live in Royal Tunbridge Wells. I haven't the foggiest idea what happened to my brothers and sisters but I do think I have been awfully lucky with my People. They go to a lot of trouble to make sure I am happy and comfortable. I have the best dog food, (from Wolfitt's, don't you know), that money can buy for breakfast and tea – none of your Pedigree Chum slop! After my morning constitution I have a dental stick and then a joint stick after my final walk in the evening. My People pay for me to be taken out daily by Angie, my dog walker (more on her and the pack later) and I have my own sofa to sleep on. All my jabs are up to date, kennel cough and flu booster, I have a bath, grooming and teeth brushing sessions on a regular basis, monthly flea and worm preventative treatments always accompanied by a bone and am cuddled all of the time.

The other people, the children, are minor characters in the drama that is my life. Their most irritating habit is to blame their wind on me – not funny! They are affectionate towards me but do not love me the way that Mummy and Daddy love me. For example, they argue with each other as to who gets to hold my lead and whose turn it is to scoop my poop. Although I have noticed when He and She Who Must Be Obeyed walk me it is always Mummy who gets to scoop my poop while He insists on holding my lead.

The other characters you will meet along the way.

Time for a snooze, methinks.

# CHAPTER 2

## *The Early Days*

Although I do not recall the exact day my People came for me, Mummy assures me it was 3 October 2004. What I do remember is that they arrived with the person who was to become my biggest sister. They stated they were looking for a dog as opposed to a bitch – He Who Must Be Obeyed muttered something under his breath about there being enough bitches in the house already and then laughed. I don't think Mummy heard him. She certainly did not laugh. The Breeder got all four of us boys out. My brothers were very sleepy having just fed. Because I'd fed from my Birth Mother first, I'd already had a little snooze and was feeling inquisitive about the visitors. I remember the lady (my Mummy) sitting on the floor. She put her hand out towards me and I scampered towards her and gently nibbled on her knuckle. It made her laugh and she picked me up and nuzzled my face with her chin. This caused me to lick her face which made her laugh even more and she then tickled me behind my ears in the way I have continued to adore and so I became a part of the family. A key part as it turns out.

Money changed hands and along with my pedigree certificate off we went. It was only when we were in the car that my People realized they had nothing for me. No collar, no lead, bed, food or anything. They didn't even have a name but called me 'Nibbler' for the time being. I began to wonder how prepared for my arrival they actually were – they have made up for it since and ensured they have catered for my every need.

As for my name, Fella, it is does not have the posh ring of a 'George' or 'Theakston' and does hark back to my Essex roots I suppose. Mummy heard Daddy talking on the phone one day to someone from work and every other word was, 'Alright Fella,' and, 'Nice one Fella,' and finally, 'See ya' Fella,' and that's how my name was born. As Mummy heard the word over and over, it played around in her head.

"That's it! Fella! That's who you are, because you're a real boy!" She was happy so I was happy. I suppose it could have been worse. Three of my pedigree friends have been named Sir Chomps – A – Lot, Baron Von Furrypants and Sir Meaty of the Hills, respectively, by their crass owners. I ask you! So 'nouveau riche'! Then of course there's the Afghans (more on them later) but their respective 'nom de plumes' are Stinkie McStinkerson and Loofers O'Farrell – their people are Irish. At the other end of the village, what I like to call the Paris Hilton end, there is Audrey Shepburn, a pretty young Collie and Yager Myster Baby Puppins, a cross-dressing Chihuahua who stereotypically travels in his mistress's fake Gucci handbag.

It was only when I arrived at my new home that I realized I would never see my old home again, nor my Birth Mother or Birth brothers and sisters and I began to feel a little sad. I explored each room and left my little identifying marks at regular intervals like Hansel and Gretel did with the bread crumbs, except Daddy did not like my little markers.

The first night was the worst. I had been used to snuggling up against my Birth Mother's side, her warm chocolate brown flank protecting me from harm, scrunched in on all sides by my chubby snuffling siblings. Mummy (although at that stage she was simply She Who Must Be Obeyed) tried to make my first night as comfortable as possible. On the way home, we stopped at a supermarket where they had bought me a basket which, although for a puppy, was still enormous for me. She snuggled a fleecy blanket around me and placed the basket on the floor next to her side of the bed. She had placed her little bedside clock in the basket next to me which I thought rather odd, but as she lay in bed with her arm stretched out towards me stroking me to sleep, I listened to the gentle rhythmic ticking and as my eyes began to droop, I imagined it was my Birth Mother's heartbeat next to me. Perhaps things would be OK after all.

My People did not know a great deal about puppies. They thought it was OK to walk me round the block before I had had the rest of my jabs – I was exhausted! They decided getting a cage for me to eat and sleep in was cruel and so I had to try to remember where I went to eat and to find somewhere quiet and enclosed if I felt sleepy during the day. My favourite place was the narrow gap between the side of the sofa and the wall. The only way they could tell I was there was from the tip of my tail sticking out.

Eventually they got the hang of it, but what they had not understood was that puppies can be quite destructive. How was I to know that the place where she kept her money was off limits? As I chewed my way through the small pieces of brown and blue papers, I spotted a lovely picture of Mummy on a little pink plastic card. I licked her face because I had grown to love her by then, but couldn't help sinking my teeth, which were beginning to fall out and hurt, into the card itself. Later, after she had calmed down, I heard her make several phone calls: One to somewhere called a bank about needing a new card and another to the DVLA about possibly needing a new driving license, whatever that is. I think she was more concerned the brown and blue pieces of paper might hurt my tummy. "Well that's fifty quid I'll never see again," she grumbled. After that, I noticed that all sorts of objects were placed out of reach: bins, laundry baskets, Mummy's handbag to name but a few.

At that stage, I looked somewhat different to the way I look now. I had paws the size of dinner plates at the end of short stubby legs. My tail was thin and pointy and wagged non-stop. My ears were the size of Dumbo's and sat awkwardly on either side of my peanut shaped head and my snout was still waiting to grow long and distinguished like a true Labrador's. Instead I had a little button nose that sat below two huge blue pools that watched her every move. Across my body, fold after fold of pink hairy flesh lay waiting for my body to grow into it, which it did soon enough. My People always say, 'He didn't stay little for long.' They say it with a certain wistfulness and I wonder if they wished I had not grown quite so big quite so fast. I used to love the way they blew raspberries on my hairless pink belly.

Now, my legs are long and lean, my head has grown up between my ears, my blue eyes turned into liquid brown and my tail is so thick and long, it can clear a coffee table or fell a Christmas tree with one swipe.

*This is me on the first day at the Wade household, my new home. I was so little Mummy could pick me up with one hand. Now, my feet from toe to ankle are bigger than hers!*

# CHAPTER 3

## *My Routines*

Technically speaking, I have three sets of routines:

1. Term time during the week

2. Term time at the weekend

3. School holidays

From the above you may gather that She Who Must Be Obeyed must not only be obeyed at home but at work too for she is a teacher. I am not quite sure what she teaches. I have been to her school before, but more on that later.

In term time during the week the Mad One – this is Mummy's last born gets up at 5.15 a.m. On the one hand this is most convenient as it means I am fed. But on the other hand, 5.15 a.m. is too early, even for me! Each day I have to send them the signals of hunger by jumping up and down and running around in circles to indicate my excitement at their appearance and therefore the imminent arrival of my breakfast. Rather demeaning but it gets a result. My People have timed me eating and claim that it takes me less than thirty seconds to empty my Arsenal bowl. I don't see what's wrong with that. This is followed by a long drink at my water bowl. Mummy says I remind her of a horse when I am drinking, especially when I move my head away drooling water everywhere. Don't see it myself. Daddy says I remind him of someone called Lennie in some book about men and mice. He says I drink like him and think like him and I'm not too bright like him either. Charming!

I then settle back into bed for a snooze until it is time to go for my morning prowl. My People, especially Mummy, calls it 'Walkies'. Highly embarrassing – and she's meant to be educated. Lately, she has taken to escorting me which I am pleased about. It used to be the Mad One's job but she didn't take me very far and I didn't get a chance to do all the necessaries. This worried Mummy that I might have to cross my legs until Angie's arrival. So she takes me now and we go all the way up Canterbury Road and along Hastings Road before heading home. It is not quite the long walk that I'd like. This aspect has often baffled me: she takes me for a walk but then does not let me check out all the different scents and smells. Whose walk is it?

As we head home I hurry as I know a treat awaits me: The Dental Stick – or rather half a dental stick – it used to be a whole one and then about two years ago a busybody of a vet who thought she knew it all said I was getting 'Porky'! Cheek. So everything went down to half rations. More water before I await the Leave Taking. This is the worst part of my day. I hate Mummy's school bags and suits. They mean long hours apart. Just before she goes, she says the same thing every day. "You're in charge. You're on guard. Be a good boy with Angie and don't go running off. Come back safe to Mummy." She gives me a last kiss on the nose, scratches behind my ears and heads out of the door. Since the beginning of September, I have taken to following her out into the hallway, looking forlornly at her, adding to both our miseries. Once the door is shut, I run into the front room and stand by the window. She looks through from outside and waves at me, blowing a kiss, and then she is gone. I slope off back to my bed and take position: on guard and in charge. It is tiring though and soon I can feel my eyelids closing and I am soon... zzzzz.

Several hours later, I hear the front door go. In my half-awake state, I think it must be Mummy, but I hear Angie's voice and off I go to run with the pack.

Angie is not like Mummy. She is very kind to me, like Mummy, but she trusts me to be off my lead and to walk where she tells me to walk. She really MUST be obeyed! I jump into the back of her car and notice that Oscar the Spaniel is there, as are Jo-Jo and Lexie the Golden Labradors. We wag our tails at each other and sniff our hellos. Soon we stop to pick up, Saffy the Great Dane and Max the Retriever and then we're off. My favourite is Hargate Forest. My People take me there too sometimes. We dogs love the forest and run wildly together our necks on each other's as we run, trying to nibble each other on the scruff of the neck. There is so much to sniff and wee on at Hargate.

A couple of hours later Angie is seeing me through my front door again. I do a quick sniff and search of the downstairs to see if we have been invaded before I slurp at my water bowl again. Good to be home and have a quiet snooze before they all start arriving.

The Mad One is usually the first to arrive back. I think it is fair to say I am ecstatic to see her as I am STARVING!!!!!!! She quickly throws the food into my bowl before I have her leg off. Thus fed I slurp again and settle down for a snooze until Mummy and Daddy come home.

My People work long hours and it is often late when they return. I cannot settle until they are back and listen out for their cars to arrive and pull in, the car doors slamming and then their familiar steps along the pavement and up the steps. I am always there at the door, ready to sooth and cuddle. Mummy usually puts her bags down and puts her arms round my neck, burying her face in my fur even before she is in the house. This is a moment of bliss. We are reunited. Whatever stress was on her brow has diminished. She is calm again. I am doing everyone a service here. Once, I was late getting to the door and she was over the threshold before she could be soothed. My goodness what a foul mood she was in – with everybody! I stayed out of the way. Eventually she saw me and knelt down for a cuddle. I felt it was safe to reciprocate and watched her mood melt away. I have a gift. Daddy usually bends down to me and puts his arm round my neck before planting a kiss on top of my head. He too seems to de-stress during this exchange.

The next few hours are spent having my last walk of the evening – again Mummy has started doing this also as she needs time to unwind and gives me a longer walk to do all the necessaries. I stride home knowing a joint – sorry, half a joint stick awaits me upon my return. Long slurp of water, half of which is then drooled across the floor. I then sit and stare, unblinking, at my People as they eat their dinner, waiting for any morsels. Usually, Mummy is the only one who can see her way clear to saving me anything – hence the reason she is (secretly) my favourite human.

After this I settle down while Mummy does her school work for a few hours and then at 9 p.m. she says, "Time for bye-byes," (which I think means bedtime) and, "'Jamas time," (which seems to mean that when my collar is off I am wearing my pyjamas) and finally she stands before my sofa bed and says, "Alley – up!" (which is my cue to jump up onto my bed, turn round and round and then sit upright.) Mummy then sits down next to me, I note that not only is my head now twice the size of her 'pea head', but when we are both sitting side by side like this, I am considerably taller than her. As she puts her arms around me, she ducks under my ear, which she strokes. She says it feels and looks like soft black velvet. I finally lie down and she covers me with my 'blankie'. Every night she says: "Night night, sleep tight. See you in the morning, but not too early." I think I am the son she never had. Just before she goes to bed, she comes in to check on me and smiles when she hears me snorting and snoring contentedly. It's not a bad life, but the weekends are better and the holiday time better still!

The main difference with the weekend is that my People get up a bit later, although it is usually Mummy who gets up to feed me, worried that I am fading away or crossing my legs. Often in the mid-morning they go out – not sure where exactly. They always say they are 'going hunting' and return with lots of full carrier bags. Sometimes I know they are fibbing as I smell no food in those bags. But at the weekend I get a bone on a Friday night and again on Saturday night – that is the best time. Then I settle down in bed with a full belly and dream of running with the pack.

*Out for the count... zzzzzz but still with one eye open, on guard and in charge.*

# CHAPTER 4

## *Holiday Adventures*

The time when I am happiest is during the six weeks holiday. I know it is coming because the weather has started to get warmer and I am shedding fur to the point where my People threaten to set about me with the Dyson! Fortunately, they have never seen the need to dress me in one of those silly dog coats or sweaters that other owners subject their pets to. Hello? Haven't they noticed the fur?

Mummy is also more relaxed as I hear her counting down the days to freedom. The first week is usually spent with the children which is nice enough but both Mummy and I are absolutely ecstatic when the front door closes in the morning of the second week (when they are gone) and we stand in the hallway listening to the silence of the house and we all, me, Mummy and the house breathe a sigh of relief!

I love this time as Mummy always has plans for us. Our favourite is to go to Rockanore Beach in Hastings. When she first took me to Hastings I was a little neurotic as the word on the street was that this particular town was best avoided, especially after dark. But actually, I found the other dogs and their People rather friendly. Two summers ago we went there on the hottest day of the year. We found a perfect spot in amongst the rocks and settled ourselves down. When it got too hot, we would paddle at the water's edge and cool our feet. I can swim, don't you know, but only in lakes where there are edges to the water. I first learnt to swim on my second birthday with my cousin Thierry. It was amazing! My People were very proud of me as I paddled my legs round and around in the water. The best bit is climbing out of the water and running up to someone and shaking water all over them and hearing them scream!

I am not brave enough to swim in the sea, I do not like the way the sea rushes towards me and I am not convinced Mummy could save me if I ran into difficulties. However, she cups water in her hands and pours it over my back. Once cool, we pad back to our nest of rocks and settle down. Mummy closes her eyes and listens to her little red box, I think she calls it an iPod. I rest my head on her leg and when I am sure we are safe I feel my eyes close and before long we are both in a deep sleep. I am still on guard, however, and am alert to the slightest sound. At some point on this trip we get lunch – fish and chips for Mummy and a sausage for me. Later, we walk along the beach and back to the old fishermen's huts. There is a fantastic ice cream parlour and we always stop to get a 99 for Mummy and an ice cream in a cone for me. I do try to lick this politely, but given half a chance will turn my snout and get my jaws around the entire whip of ice cream and down in one! Cold rush to the head though!

We usually walk up many steps to the country park. It is a particularly exciting part of the trip full of wonderful scents and the odd discarded chip and morsel of fish. I am not allowed off my lead up here as Mummy says if I were to run too far to the edge there is a steep cliff so she walks me down the middle. We sit on a bench at the top and look out over the sea. Bliss! If we are not too tired we might stop off at Alexandra Park on the way back. After this we are both exhausted. I climb into the back of the car and before Mummy has even got into third gear I am asleep. It has been a lovely day, just the two of us. By the time we get home we stagger up the steps to the front door. It is almost tea time so Mummy gives me half the usual amount given that I have had a sausage and an ice cream earlier. I follow this with an enormous drink at my water bowl and then that is me for the day...

*This is me on that hot summer day in August on Rockanore Beach, looking out to sea, handsome and rugged!*

# CHAPTER 5

## *School Daze*

For some reason, still unknown to me, Mummy decided I would accompany her to school one day in early July. It was one of the more weird experiences of my life so far. Although I had done all the necessaries before we left, when we arrived, there were so many new smells and sounds that I needed to go all over again. Also, I was fairly nervous. In a mad moment, I wondered if Mummy was trying to tell me something and that this was to be my new home. The scooper was used several times, much to Mummy's embarrassment. Her school is most peculiar. In fact, I could not work out if it was a school, a farm or a zoo. They have sheep there and most aggressive they were too. As soon as they saw me I heard them making plans to ambush me later with the cows! That made me jump and Mummy called me a 'Wus', whatever that is – I think it means 'Wonderful Under Stress.'

She had brought her first born with us to look after me while she taught. Mummy does not appear to have a classroom. Every lesson was taken outside on the field whilst I and Firstborn sat under a tree. Summer and black

Labradors do not mix and I was grateful for the shade. Her students were either deranged or smelt odd and some had both characteristics. I still can't work out what Mummy teaches – wrestling, perhaps. Her students were doing some sort of fighting exercise. At this point, I was still unsure as to why I was there and was wondering what the Pack was doing and if the house was safe without me there to guard it. When the postman delivered and realized I was not there defending the territory, he would probably tell all of his acquaintances who would be round there like a shot, purloining everything they could lay their hands on. Just hoped I wouldn't get the blame.

Later that day Mummy took me inside. I was a bit worried about this as this establishment is not particularly Fella friendly. There were tiled or wood floors everywhere! What was I supposed to stand on without skidding everywhere? Fortunately, we were taken to the Drama Studio, which turned out to be Mummy's proper classroom, where someone had put down a pathway of carpet for me to walk on. How convenient, I thought. A few hours later, what I think was the real purpose of my visit became apparent. I was to be the guest star of Mummy's assembly. I could hear this murmur of noise and Mummy's voice, talking about me and then on cue, First Born led me out of the Drama Studio and onto the stage, where a similar network of carpet awaited me. The murmur turned to hushed silence and a few 'Ahh's. As Firstborn led me along the path I saw Mummy waiting at the centre of the stage by my basket – how did that come to be there? I noticed also my Arsenal bowl and my brush and toothbrush. Perhaps I was moving out after all. And then I spotted them – a whole hall full of people, looking at me! I tried to be brave and wagged my tail a little. Mummy scratched behind my ears and carried on talking to the children about me and our adventures together. She slipped a biscuit into my mouth and I crunched it noisily and gratefully, less nervous now.

During the assembly, I stood patiently while Mummy demonstrated how she groomed me and brushed my teeth. I held my perfect pedigree Labrador pose, back legs slightly extended, shoulders forward, head up and snout pointing northwards. I jumped into my basket and let her cover me up to demonstrate our bedtime routine. I have to admit, by this stage I was so exhausted, I could have done with forty winks. But a performance is a performance and the show must go on. There was a further assembly to do to the other half of the school and I fought the temptation to do any necessaries on the stage or to bite the little oiks in the front row who kept hissing at me.

My work day was not over yet, however, and in the afternoon I got to sit in the corner of Mummy's classroom on a rug in a pool of sunlight while, one by one, different children came and sat down on the bean bag next to me and quietly read to me. The theory is that being a canine, I will listen to them patiently, without trying to correct them and helping them to build their confidence. This worked, up to a point, but by the time I'd got the eighth reader in front of me I was so tired from performing in assembly that I fell asleep while Jordan was reading to me and began snoring heavily, much to his classmates' amusement and Jordan's distress.

Despite these trials, I was handsomely rewarded with one bone and six biscuits and by the time I climbed into the back of the car was feeling a little on the nauseous side and grateful for my long awaited snooze all the way home.

Once home I was too tired even to check the house for intruders, but dragged myself under the coolness of the dining room table and remained there until 5 p.m. that evening when I woke, an hour late, for my tea!

# CHAPTER 6

## *The Pembury Massive*

It is a truth universally acknowledged that dogs are either friendly or downright nasty. I am one of the former but have the misfortune to live in a village with several of the latter. In the past, I have been attacked by:

1. The Afghans – Stinkie and Loofers – They come as a pair, one black, the other sandy coloured but both nasty bullies who think nothing of surrounding me so that I am cornered and take it in turns to bite me on the bum. Their owner is a pensioner who has no control over them whatsoever. He Who Must Be Obeyed had to kick the sandy one in the side to get him off me.

2. Toby the Devil Dog (aka Toblerone) – Toby belongs to the Vicar ironically, but neither of his owners can control him. Toby is a Golden Labrador crossed with something psycho as every time he sees me he rears up on his hind legs, growling and snarling and his owners have to literally brace their feet against a hedge to stop him from pulling them over. Toby chased me once over the fields, must have been when I was two. He cornered me against a bush and I snarled back at him and lunged towards him. A

bit of a risky strategy that, as I had no idea if he would back down – but he did and Mummy and Daddy were very proud of me and gave me extra biscuits.

3. Lolita – the Alsatian who is completely feral and the choice of name is a dead giveaway! Lolita and I arrived as puppies in Pembury around the same time in 2004. Unfortunately, Lolita did not live with a good family and they allowed her to escape and forage for food all of the time. The last time I saw Lolita, I was just arriving at the fields and still on my lead. She came tearing around the corner and went straight for me. The next thing I saw was a black and sandy blur as she went flying at the end of Mummy's boot. I was very proud of Mummy, who was as terrified of Lolita as I was and I gave her extra licks (or tried to).

4. Blue – he is a mongrel – it has to be said. He is a rescue dog and is owned by a pensioner who cannot control him. He should be muzzled as every time he sees me, he tears across the field to attack me. It never fails to amaze me that he forgets that every time he does this, he comes into sharp contact with Daddy's steel-capped boot. Daddy is my hero! He would never let anything horrible happen to me.

5. The Rottweilers – These two do not live together but go for walks together which is a big mistake as it makes every other dog in the field dive into the nearest bush until they have passed – except Toby, who is psycho, remember. Their owners, a couple of ladies (one a pensioner – see a pattern here?) say that they are pussycats! I say, 'No, they are eating machines who would rip my head off at the first opportunity.'

6. Random nutter cum Bull Terrier types. – These have increased in number during my eight years here in Pembury and I have yet to meet one that did not have trouble on his mind.

7.   Tyson – I must not forget Tyson – sounds like a huge monster but he is, in fact, a scrawny Yorkshire Terrier who nips at my ankles every opportunity he gets.

8.   Two full size Huskies – know very little about them except that they would probably give the two Rotties a run for their money.

The answer has been, therefore, for my owners to arm themselves with a metal bat, like a rounders bat. They take a ball with them in case they are accused of carrying an offensive weapon, but really it is to beat the living daylights out of any of these psycho dogs that roam the ironically named Harmony Playing fields, should they try to take a pop at me. I have to admit, I feel more confident when Daddy is carrying the bat. He is stronger and I feel would defend me more fully than Mummy could. Mummy is more useful for me to stand behind while Daddy does the fighting. It's a jungle out there I tell you.

*And I'm King of it!*

# CHAPTER 7

## *The Pembury Crew*

The Pembury Crew are the good guys (and gals), many of whom are part of Angie's pack. We are the friendly dogs who are kind to each other, playful, devoted to our Owners and just want a peaceful life. My friends include:

1.    Lexie – Golden Labrador – who lives with Angie. She has a particular fancy for me and will often run across the fields with me, nibbling at my ears and neck.

2.    Jo-Jo – Golden Labrador – also lives with Angie – the elder of the two who likes me but prefers Harley to me – I think it is because he still has his Man Parts.

3.    Sam – elderly Golden Retriever – not part of the pack but lives in Pembury and we see each other regularly on our road walks. Plods along and then becomes quite skittish when he sees me, which is nice.

4.    Charlie – Charlie is my new best friend – he is a year old black working Cocker Spaniel and has a lovely sense of fun. When we meet on our road walks, he always stops to jump up and put his paws round my neck. I think secretly, Mummy would like to have a Charlie as well as a

Fella at home. He has beautiful soft brown eyes which look lovingly up at me.

5.   Harley – or Harley Farley as Mummy calls him. He is a five year old Vissler who has just moved to Horsmonden, so I don't see him so much anymore. He and I grew up together, although I never liked the way he nipped at my neck just a bit too hard for my liking. And he used to slobber all over me.

6.   Saffy – a massive Great Dane. I love Saffy, but she just takes up too much space in the back of the car and if she's had sprouts the night before... She too has commandeered a human chair in her house (see below).

7.   Tilly – eighteen month old Golden Labradoodle – great fun for a girl.

8.   Woody – a five year old Weimarana – very shy since he was attacked a couple of years ago. He and I were caught out in a snow blizzard a few years ago with our Mummies. It was great fun!

9.   Lucy – I must add little Lucy to the list – she was Angie's Doberman and my girlfriend. Lucy and I were both timid but I did my best to look after her when we were out. I found out a few months ago that Lucy was not well and then one day, she wasn't there anymore. Lexie and Jo-Jo said very little and from that I took to understand that she had passed on. Angie was very upset when I heard her tell Mummy and Daddy. Mummy had tears in her eyes and was very quiet for the rest of the day, except to give me extra cuddles now and again. It reminded me of that time when she and Daddy went out one evening with Auntie Karen and Uncle Liam leaving our First Born and their Second Born in charge of me and Thierry (more on him later). When they came back, Mummy had definitely been crying and even Daddy's eyes looked a little pink. She burst through the door and threw her arms around me, hugging me tightly. Afterwards, I

heard it was to do with something called a 'Marley and Me' – No idea.

10. Thierry is my cousin – named after the famous Thierry Henry because his Daddy also is an Arsenal supporter – I thought I had it bad with the collar and the dog bowl – however, it does sound a rather distinguished name! He is a five year old black Labrador though, they say he is an American type – not sure what that means as he doesn't have an accent but he is not as stocky (Daddy says fat!) as me and has had lots of problems with his knees. Thierry and I are great pals and once we have had our mad half hour, we usually settle down for a snooze and food watch.

*I ought to mention here that Thierry has the added advantage over me of having a Mummy who will let him lick her face, as she lets me do every time I see her, whenever he wants. Trouble is, he chooses not to – Bizarre! Perhaps she could see her way clear to persuading Mummy to let me do the same.*

*My friend Saffy at home (literally) in her armchair.*

# CHAPTER 8

## *Annoying Habits (Me)*

Like humans, we dogs have our own faults and foibles. Over the years I have come to discover those of my habits that my People find particularly annoying or, in some cases, downright disgusting. Top of the list has to be:

1.    Eating poo – mine or anybody else's. I try to do it surreptitiously, but they always catch me. Cat's poo is the best. They regularly deposit in the front garden and if I'm lucky, I can get to it before my lead is even on. But if I'm caught they get ever so cross. I get a smacked bottom, my teeth brushed and no treats. Even Mummy, who usually adores me finds this trait particularly unacceptable. I have tried hard not to, but sometimes, I just get a whiff of fresh poo, and I cannot help myself.

2.    Humping my basket – my People thought this would stop when they had my Man Parts chopped off, but I still like to give the old basket a good thrusting from time to time. I never quite know what has come over me but it usually coincides with seeing some pretty bitch at some point that day. My basket has gone up in the loft now as it

took up too much room and my People were embarrassed one day when I humped it in front of Nana.

3.    Staring – now the jury is split on this one. Daddy hates me doing this, especially while he's eating, whereas, Mummy does not seem to mind so much. I think she loves the sense of devotion she feels I am imparting through my stare, whether I am sitting staring at her or lying by her feet staring up at her. Either way, I am always rewarded for my patience by a scrap of food or a tickle behind my ears and three kisses on my forehead. I just have to be careful that the stare is not accompanied by:

4.    The dribble – I have to confess this is unpleasant if you are trying to eat. The long stream of drool is enough to put anyone off their meal and that doesn't necessarily mean that said meal ends up in my tummy, because it doesn't!

5.    Ripping up my bedding – when my basket went up into the loft, I inherited the old sofa in the conservatory. It's a three seater and fairly battered, but it's mine. Trouble is I can't quite get the sofa cushions how I want them unless I just rearrange the stuffing and that involves ripping open the cover and pulling the stuffing out with my claws, trampling it around the sofa, round and round and squashing it down with my bottom. The problem is the next day when Mummy comes in and sees my handiwork. She never quite gets what it was I was trying to achieve. She says I'm destructive and must be cross about something. Other days she says I'm depressed and reacting to the stress in the house. Actually, all I'm trying to do is get a decent night's sleep! It's all very well for them, they have a lovely big King size bed to sleep in, with lovely pillows and a duck feather filled 13.5 tog duvet over them.

6.    General hairiness – now this one really is not my fault. I am black, I am a Labrador, I am, by my very nature, hairy and I moult – in the summer when it's hot and in the winter when the central heating is on. So pretty much all

year round. They clearly didn't do their research and they have a Dyson, for Heaven's sake!

7.   I am worried that I am already on no. 7 – Am I really that annoying? Well number 7 is my sudden loud barking. Mummy says I am barking at thin air (whatever that might be). What I am actually doing is guarding. If I sense something, I will bark regardless of the fact that it caused Mummy to spill her soup the other day. Very nice too it was. It is embarrassing and a little annoying when she opens the front door to show me that I am barking at nothing. Then I DO feel a bit foolish.

8.   Farting – All I will say is that they have been described as silent and deadly and on occasions I have been re-named 'Beanfart of Pembury'.

9.   Waking my People up early – I think this is a natural thing to be up and awake at 6 a.m. day in day out. Apparently, Mummy has been talking to Auntie Karen, who says Thierry, lazy git, sleeps in until 8.30 a.m.!

10. Licking Mummy's face – now many would see this, not as an annoying habit, but as something rather endearing. She says it is my fishy breath that makes it annoying! That and if I have been doing annoying habit no. 1!

*I have been known to hold this unblinking stare for 43 minutes and 32 seconds, especially if it is a roast dinner in the offing.*

# CHAPTER 9

## *Annoying Habits (Them)*

1.   Making me wait – for food, for walks, in fact for anything.

2.   Not letting me sleep on the leather sofas – something to do with my claws and the mess I have made with the sofa in the conservatory.

3.   The Annoying One irritating my feet when I am asleep, or lying all over me.

4.   The other Annoying One taking both my ears in her hands and lifting them up in the air as she says, "Chihuahua."

5.   Leaving me at the weekend to go off 'hunting' and then not coming back with any food.

6.   Putting the washing machine on at 10 p.m. when I am trying to go to sleep. Do they not know how noisy that final spin is?

7.   Telling everyone what a scaredy cat I am. To be called any kind of cat is the highest insult. So what if I

cower when people run past me or click their automatic car locks as I walk by?

8.    When they stroke or tickle me for a few minutes and then think they can just stop! I usually raise my paw onto their arm to encourage them to continue (which they say is annoying – no. 11?) or I nudge them with my nose (which they also say is annoying – no. 12?)

9.    Making me wear an Arsenal collar – the bowl I can at least hide from the general public.

10.    Making me wear a halter when travelling in the back of the car – a necessary evil, I realize, but annoying nonetheless and I invariably end up nearly strangling myself.

11.    Talking for me. Do any of you other dogs out there have People who pretend to speak your thoughts? For example:

He Who Must Be Obeyed: (In exaggerated posh voice that is supposed to be me) "Er Daddy, do you think you could see your way clear to allowing me up onto the leather sofas?"

He Who Must be Obeyed: (In his own voice) "I don't think so do you?"

He Who Must Be Obeyed: (In exaggerated posh voice that is supposed to be me) "But Daddy, I would be far more comfortable up there and there would then be less hair on the floor."

He Who Must be Obeyed: (In his own voice) "Ah, you're not going to fool me like that my boy."

Sometimes both He and She Who Must Be Obeyed carry out this ridiculous two way conversation between themselves! It is truly irritating.

*The food was late arriving and had been in my Arsenal bowl for approximately 12 seconds. I love a good scoff don't you know.*

# CHAPTER 10

## *Medical History*

I was born one night on 12 August 2004. I do not recall there being any medical intervention. I dare say the Breeders did all the work along with my Birth Mother, Flakes Surprise. I remember very little about my Birth Mother but have heard Mummy say she was an enormous chocolate brown Labrador, mad as a March hare, whatever that is, and my Birth Father a black Labrador, who was clearly not the wearer of the trousers in that relationship. I am hoping they were metaphorical trousers and that my father did not have People who made him dress up!

From the time my People got me home on 3 October 2004, they have made sure I have always had my injections and boosters at Dacre House Veterinary Surgery. The vets there are very kind and have always had a soft spot for me. I think it is because I do not try to bite them when they examine me. What I do not like about the practice is the flooring – all tiles. How do they expect me to walk on that? I am scared of non-carpeted surfaces – wood, tiles, laminate, linoleum. If it's not a rug or a carpet (preferably shag pile) then I'm up the proverbial creek without a paddle – like Bambi on ice. Mummy and Daddy discovered this themselves one day when they ripped up all of the carpets in the house and spent thousands of pounds on laminate flooring only to find that I could not walk on any of it. So off they went to spend hundreds of pounds on rugs and runners – just for me. They must love me very much.

Getting into the car to go to the vets is always very exciting and my excitement continues even when we get there. For some reason, the nerves take over when Mummy opens the front door and I have to walk in. Then I put my tail under my back legs, my claws try to grip the floor and I try to make a dash for the car.

Most of the time, I am there just for a booster which they inject into the scruff of my neck. They also check my teeth, my heart rate, my coat, all of which they find in good condition. Occasionally, I am dragged through to stand on the scales. Most of the time, I am 'overweight'. What they do not understand is that I have very heavy fur, lots and lots of it. So for the few days after this judgement, my People put me on half rations but by the weekend Mummy has usually buckled and I'm back to my usual amount.

Twice I have had to stay at the vets for an operation. The first time was to remove my Man Parts. Apparently, this was to calm me down. I thought I was perfectly calm. So what if I didn't always come back when I ran off over the fields? So what if I humped everything in sight? So what if I kept jumping on everything and everyone? To this day I still find it awkward when meeting and greeting other dogs; each goes straight to the other's backside, sizing up the goods or checking out their absence. I am sure this is why the Pembury Massive attack me, or try to – They all still have their Man Parts.

I have had other treatments: removal of a wart, removal of a growth on my eye, eye infections, poorly tummy, muscle strain in my leg (though this was faked in order to get more attention – how was I to know they'd whisk me off to the vet's?)

One Sunday, last summer, Mummy thought I was dying. It was a hot day and she and Daddy were sitting at the patio table. I was sat at their feet. Daddy scraped his chair which made me jump and skid on the patio stones. This scared me and I couldn't move for fear of skidding again. They thought I had hurt myself and Daddy picked me up like a shepherd picking up a sheep (all seven stone of me – very impressive) and put me down on my bed. I don't know why but I was making a growling noise which Mummy interpreted as me not breathing properly and she went into panic mode, dialling the vet and phoning the emergency number. She was all for whisking me down there onto their operating table. I mistook this for a walk and leapt off the sofa clearly in the peak of health at which point I overheard her saying: "Can you give me a minute? I just want to double check him. Can I get back to you in ten minutes?"

That's when I knew I'd been found out. Fortunately, Mummy was more relieved than cross and gave me extra cuddles. Funny that I don't get the same reaction when she is cross with me for eating poo… Apart from that I am generally a healthy specimen with none of the usual design faults such as hips dysplasia and I put that down to the lovely food, walks and love that I get. It's not a bad life.

*Mummy's Boy!*

# CHAPTER 11

## *The Jeskyns Boys*

Occasionally during the school holidays, Mummy takes me to Jeskyns Country Park where she meets up with her friends Karen (not to be mistaken for Auntie Karen) and Caroline. Karen brings her boy Ben, an elderly golden Labrador and Caroline brings her boy Buddy a two year old chocolate Labrador. We are an interesting mix. Benny and I are older and wiser and, being without our Man Parts, somewhat calmer than Buddy who is still rather feisty.

At Jeskyns, we frolic together, chasing after balls, swimming in the Doggy Pond and generally running together. Ben tires the soonest and I, now at seven and middle-aged, am grateful for the opportunity to walk quietly next to him from time to time. Ben has given me some good advice before regarding the warning signs of growing old. I, in turn, have tried to pass some of my own wisdom onto young Buddy, but he never stays still long enough to hear it. I envy him his youth and his ability to run and run. And the fact he still has his Man Parts.

One good thing about being a three dog mission is that

no other dog messes with us when we are at Jeskyns. The only real threat is Buddy as Benny is too old to fight, I am too scared to fight and even Buddy has the attention span of a mosquito and would forget to fight, if it came to it.

The other good thing about this three man mission is the triple treats available from each of the Mummies. We are like bees to the proverbial honey pot.

*This is my friend Ben. Buddy wouldn't stay still long enough to have his photo taken. Ben is brave – Note the vast expanse of laminate he is able to walk on!*

# CHAPTER 12

## *'Tis The Season To Be Jolly…*

We are in the season of Advent as I write, and like all good Mummies, she has bought me my own advent calendar, so it's a half dental stick in the morning, and a chocolate (suitable for me) before she goes to work (or for my elevenses at the weekend). Auntie Karen also bought me an advent calendar so I have another chocolate in the evening. I also have my own Christmas stocking which Father Christmas (aka wonderful Mummy) fills with all my favourite scrummy treats and presents under the tree. I'm not sure how accurate I have been, but I do believe I have counted out more presents for me this year than for any one of the children!

Like last year, we have snow this year. I love snow, being a Canadian breed, and love to push my face through it as I run along. This makes my People laugh and say I look like Father Christmas. Today, we went for a long walk around the village which was fairly uneventful apart from a random Pit-bull type nutter and then a bus, which changed gear and made a whooshing noise as it passed us. This made me jump and I crouched down low and tried to turn back the way I had come. Mummy crouched down low next to me and put her arms around me and her face close to mine.

"It's OK, Fells. I'll look after you. It's only a bus. You're OK." I had hoped she would call me a 'Wus' as I thought I was rather 'Wonderful Under Stress', but she kissed me on the head and we carried on our way. Nasty bus.

On Christmas Day itself, I woke even earlier than usual desperate to see what Father Christmas had left in my stocking. I was not to be disappointed! The most exciting present was a new, non-Arsenal collar. I say was because it turned out to be too big for me and had to go back. It has been replaced by a rather smart '3 peaks' collar, also red which contrasts beautifully with my black shiny coat and makes me look rather Tunbridge Wells trendy, you know like those people who wear Northface or Berghaus. I certainly look like a very intrepid explorer. Very posh.

I got a new green (and therefore non-Arsenal) food bowl, a new night-time collar with flashing light, a set of rubber joined rings chewy toy for me and Daddy to play rough 'n' tumble with. There was also a new blankie for me and it is soooo soft. Mummy wraps me up in it every night to keep me warm. I got lots of lovely food presents too: A dog bone, a Doggy Christmas Pudding and some gravy bones (my favourite). I waited patiently at the bottom of the stairs, my head resting on the bottom step looking up, hoping to see my People emerge from their bedroom. By my head sat their presents from me, a pair of slippers for him and a new Best Mum in the World Boofle Mug for her. I do hope they like them. They are given with my love.

The rest of Christmas Day is spent eating, walking, sleeping and waiting until it is time to do one of those three again. Daddy gets a little cross with me at one point in the day. They have laid a board down on the floor with some funny plastic things on it. I thought it was a new sleep mat for me and I plonked my bottom down in the middle of it. Mummy groaned and Daddy shouted something about 'trivial pursuit' – I couldn't agree more.

*"And lo, he was swathed in a… dog blanket!"*

# THE MIDDLE OF THE BOOK (No. 13 is unlucky)

## *New Year Resolutions*

As much as I despise those who make such promises, I feel it incumbent upon myself to lead the moral crusade in this household, having witnessed so much greed and slothishness during the festive season. And my People didn't behave much better either! I expect that if I make a few choice resolutions then maybe my People will follow suit. After all there are only so many days you can fill by eating and sleeping.

**Fella Wade's Resolutions for 2012:**

1. Eat less and exercise more

2. Try not to scare the postman so much.

3. Always sleep in my own bed every night

4. Let Mummy sleep in at the weekends

5. Walk sensibly on all shiny floors in the house

6. Stay awake more during the day

7.   Stand up for myself more against any member of the Pembury Massive

8.   Wear a Christmas bandana round my neck like Thierry

9.   Introduce myself in more appropriate ways

10.  Stop begging for scraps from Mummy's plate


OK… Well if you believe that you'll believe anything – having red through the last twelve chapters – does that really sound like me??? For your perusal I have written the real Fella Wade's Resolutions for 2012:

1.   Daddy on floor, Fella in the bed (with Mummy)

2.   Find every bone I have ever buried

3.   Stop begging and actually get a seat at the dinner table

4.   Give up the dream of ever catching my tail

5.   Give up the dream of ever seeing my Man Parts again

6.   Bark like a big dog but still get cuddled on lap like a little dog

7.   Now that I have the run of the main family sofa seek possession of one of the two new 'Cuddler' chairs.

8.   Persuade Mummy to give me a full cup of food for breakfast and dinner, a whole dental stick and a whole joint stick.

9.   Ensure that Mummy and Daddy never leave me again to go on holiday.

10. Sleep deeply at every available opportunity… ZZzzzzz.

# CHAPTER 14

## *Brain Of Britain*

"Bless, he's not the brightest…" If I had a dog biscuit for every time I had heard this said about me… well I'd be a very fat Labrador indeed. I am not a stupid boy. In fact, I am highly skilled in many ways. I have the hearing of a bat and can hear the tiniest crackle of a food packet, I can see the smallest crumb and I can smell the merest hint of food, cooked or raw from a 100 yard distance. That's pretty clever, isn't it? So I may not be the bravest, but I am devoted and would like to think I would defend Mummy if a bad man tried to attack her. Well, at least I would lick him to death and at the very least, stun him senseless with my rancid breath.

I can also recognize places. For instance, as soon as we get to the T junction in Hastings, I know we are going to turn left and park within minutes in the Rockanore Car Park. When we arrive at the roundabout in Benfleet, I know Thierry is just a few minutes away and as we go down the bumpy road on the other side of town, I know that the mud and trees of Hargate Forest beckon. That's very smart.

I know the time: when it is breakfast time, dinner time, walk time.

I know lots of words: breakfast, dinner, chicken, sausages, drink of water, bedtime, walkies, collar, alley-up, bye-byes, Mummy, Daddy, Thierry, sit, go lie down, biscuit, dental stick, joint stick, push, come on, what have I got, round the block and when Mummy spells out W-A-L-K or B-O-N-E, I know exactly what she means!

I think Mummy confuses my timidity with a lack of intelligence. I realize I would never be able to sniff out drugs (not unless they were wrapped in sausages), nor walk a blind person across the road (Daddy says I have no road sense and would probably add to the road kill if I were a Guide Dog). I have a secret envy of those assistant dogs which help those who are disabled, however, I do know that I provide a massive service to Mummy and that is the role of Chief Comforter and Pal through thick and thin. I am the only one who can cheer her up when she is down, I keep all of her secrets and listen to her when she is cross or upset. When she is happy, we smile together and walk with a synchronized bounce in our step.

There was a day when she thought she had lost me or, rather, a stupid woman had lost me. An estate agent, who I particularly disliked, was showing a couple around my home. While they were in the back garden, Angie arrived and, relieved, I bounded out of the front door after her. Stupid Estate Agent Woman thought she must have left the front door open and that I had escaped. She then left a message on Mummy's phone to say I had gone. According to Mummy's friends and Angie, Mummy looked and sounded as if something appalling had happened, as if someone had died and was so upset and relieved when she discovered I was safe, that she could not continue working. That night I remember, when she arrived home, she hugged me most of the night. Stupid Estate Agent Woman did not darken our doorstep again and our house came off the market.

*This is my Mummy helping me write my story. See what I mean about our heads??*

# CHAPTER 15

## *Centre Parcs (aka Colditz)*

A few years ago, my People were talking about a family holiday to somewhere called Centre Parcs. The two words that burnt in my brain (pea sized or not) were 'family' and 'parcs'. I was family, wasn't I? And a park is a perfect place for dogs. Before long, Mummy was telling me all about this marvellous holiday that we (me included) would be going on with Auntie Karen, Uncle Liam, their Second Born and Cousin Thierry. She spoke of a villa and forests where we two boys could run and sniff and walk to our hearts' content. It sounded perfect. It also sounded too good to be true. I began to count down the days before the time came for us all to pack into the car, with our luggage, much of which was wedged in around me as I sat in my basket in the boot of the Picasso.

The journey was long and not really to my liking. I couldn't stretch my legs or see anything out of the windows and had to remain in the same curled up position for just over two whole hours! But it would be worth it, when we got there.

Eventually we arrived at a massive wooded area, we

pulled up outside our villa to unload. Being a canine, I am not sure what constitutes a villa, but judging by the looks on my Peoples' faces, this was not it. I leapt out of the boot, shook myself and then stretched first one back leg and then the other and then, pointing my snout to the sky, stretched my neck and spine. Thus detangled, I trotted happily along the path to the front door of our 'home from home' and stopped dead: LAMINATE!!!

"Mum!" I heard the Mad One screech, "you're not gonna like this." Mummy's not going to like this? Mummy? What about me? I am certainly not going to like this. My People took one look at the floors throughout the villa and groaned. One by one, they traipsed past me with their luggage, happily moving in.

"Come on Fella," said my Mummy, as cheerfully as she could.

"Not on your Nelly!" my eyes were saying.

"It's fine, sweetie, come on." She tried to drag me in by my lead but I wasn't having any of it and put my head down and dug my feet and then my bottom into the 'Welcome' mat. Eventually, she disappeared into the villa, leaving the Sensible One (used to be the Annoying One who held my ears aloft saying Chihuahua) holding my lead at the doorway. What's happening? What's going on? Am I staying? Am I going? I was so pleased to see Mummy return.

"Right Fells, everything's OK, I've got it all sorted." Putting my complete trust in She Who Must Be Obeyed, I gingerly extended my nose around the doorway to see what miracle she had worked that would suddenly make 'everything OK'.

"That's it – look, carpets!" Never in a million years could some skanky looking blankets pass for carpets. She had run around all of the rooms to see what she could purloin. Seeing aforementioned blankets stashed away in cupboards, she knew they were far too disgusting to put over humans, so had laid them out on the laminate floor, anchoring them down with pieces of furniture. In theory this should have been fine. Unfortunately, in my nervousness, instead of walking slowly and sensibly on them, I tried to cross them as quickly as possible to reach the single rug in the centre of the room. The blankets duly slid underneath my claws, sending me scampering even faster, until I landed thud against the coffee table which also had pride of place on the rug. Even though I had entered from the front door, I had somehow managed to dislodge every blanket Mummy had carefully laid out and weighed down.

As she surveyed me trembling upon two square feet of rug, she put her head in her hands and said, "This is going to be a long week."

And so it was. Every night, I was put to bed on the sofas as I felt too scared to lie on the floor in case it moved. At some point in the middle of the night, I would get thirsty, or lonely and get up, jump down onto the floor forgetting that it was like an ice rink and then, trying to make my way across to my water bowl or Mummy and Daddy's bedroom door, would remember that it was like an ice rink. I would then stop and freeze, digging my claws in and that was when the whimpering began.

Inevitably, it was Mummy who got up to see to me. I knew that if I added in a tremble, I could persuade her to curl up on the sofa and stay with me. It didn't make for a restful week. Mummy's way of coping seemed to be to drink copious amounts of alcohol each night and end up screeching with laughter with Auntie Karen. Hmmm, can't say that I approve. Some nights they were drunk in charge of canines and it was only our fantastic sense of smell that got us home at all.

Day time was little better. The long walks and runs through the forest that were promised also came to nothing. Dogs had to be kept on leads at all times except in the dog walking areas which were approximately ten metres by ten metres. A Poodle or a Yorkshire Terrier might have been able to work up a sweat but not your full grown Labrador, oh no, definitely not!

When our People went off for the morning or afternoon to have fun, they thought it would be a good idea for us boys to be kept together. A disaster I tell you! Thierry howled and barked non-stop. I implored him to 'put a sock in it' but he was beside himself, and, more unfortunately, beside me. I lay on the sofa with my front paws firmly wedged over my ears, but nothing could block out the noise. My People, as they returned, could hear the noise from several metres away and decided that, in future, I would be better off alone when they were out. Phew! Telepathy does work. The end of the week could not have come soon enough. When we got home, I was so pleased to see the various rugs, runners and carpets, I literally drooled all over them before staggering to my bed and falling fast asleep for the first time in a week! If it looks too good to be true – it probably is!

# CHAPTER 16

## *The Alternative(s)*

On an annual basis, my People take their summer holiday, invariably to a place you can only get to by aeroplane and requiring a passport. As I can neither go on a plane nor own a passport, this requires me to be looked after by A.N.OTHER. Mostly, this has been Angie and last June was no exception.

Now as much as I adore Angie, I do not a) like being parted from Mummy and Daddy and b) being away from home for long periods (i.e. more than five hours). I knew, as Mummy walked me up to Angie's gate that something was up. For a start I had spotted her trying to secrete my basket and other bulky items out of the house late yesterday evening. Secondly, with my radar already on full alert, I realized that we weren't just going 'walkies' (still embarrassing – why can't she just say 'walk'?) but that in fact I was going to Angie's – to stay. I did my usual pulling and trying to jump up at Mummy, my tongue lolling from side to side winsomely, but she still passed my lead over to Angie, said a quick goodbye and hurried out of the gate with the welts of my scratch marks streaked down her stomach.

No amount of sun will tan those I thought smugly. If she was going to abandon me for a week, I would make her suffer. Little did I realize, I was the one to suffer.

Since my last holiday at Angie's, she had had her flooring re-done – yes, you've guessed it. Gone was the carpet and in its place shiny, slippery linoleum. 'Oh My Dog!' I thought. Angie could not understand why I would not come inside and gradually realized that the floor was the problem. She moved my basket as close as possible to the door to allow me to leap straight into it, but then what? The door needed to be closed and I was in the way. Angie is an amazing person, who clearly loves dogs and nothing was too much trouble. Firstly she tried to pull me (in my basket remember) further into the room but I wouldn't budge. Instead she stepped over me and pushed my basket from the other side until I slid into the centre of the room. The other lodgers for that week, a Spaniel, a Setter and a Retriever as well as Jo-Jo, Lexie and Lucy looked on with a mixture of amusement (Spaniels can snigger) and bemusement – this from the Setter. Jo-Jo and Lexie knew all my little foibles. Lucy, bless her, lay with her head against my basket offering as much moral support as she could.

The next day dawned bright and I was pleased when Angie came down to feed and walk us. What I was less happy with was being left in this sea of slipperiness and I barked and barked until she relented and bundled me into her car and allowed me to come with her on all of her pick-ups. Until this day, I had not appreciated that Angie walked any other dogs. I thought that once she had dropped me back at home, she just went home and put her feet up, but no, Angie walks four to five sets of dogs a day. There was the Pembury Crew, the Tonbridge Gang, the Southborough Lot and the Tunbridge Wells Consortium (This consisted of dogs in the Pantiles, St Marks, Neville Park and Warwick Park wards). This meant I walked/ran for up to eight hours every day my People were away. I had no choice, it was either that or spend an anguished few hours trembling in my basket.

When Angie finally dropped me back to my own home again, as soon as Mummy opened the door, I knocked her flying. The welts on her stomach that had begun to heal were renewed with vigour. I had her pinned to the floor in the conservatory, managing to lick her face and ears as her head writhed from side to side. I had missed them very much. Mummy noticed immediately how trim and svelte I was looking. Little did she know that I had run the equivalent of 120 miles that week!

The reason my People had placed me with Angie for that week is that the year before when they had gone away, they had trusted First Born at the age of seventeen to look after me in the house. And why not, you might ask yourself? Well, for a start, she's seventeen with the house to herself for the week, so what does that automatically mean: Paaaartttttyyyyyy! At least I think that is what I heard her scream down her little portable phone no sooner had the front door closed. Mummy had left long lists of very precise instructions as to my routine from the timings of my feeds and walks to my night time routine and what she was supposed to say to me. I can honestly say I do not recall seeing those lists all week.

The week was OK in itself. The problem was Thursday night when said 'Paaaartttttyyyyyy' was scheduled to happen. Had my People taught me how to text I would have been on the phone straight away warning them. As it is, things did not get too out of hand. Some boys were doing silly things like head stands and I was tempted to bite them on their Man Parts. The girls were nicer and I spent much of the night being tickled and stroked by a number of sweet smelling scantily clad young ladies, my head resting against their copious bosoms.

Despite the pictures on Facebook (who puts pictures of an illicit party at their parents' house whilst they are away on Facebook? Especially when said parents are listed as your 'friends'? Duh!) I can categorically deny that I was plied with alcohol of any kind that night. I am fairly confident that it was the late night which caused me to sleep so soundly and then oversleep the next day.

Needless to say, when Mummy and Daddy found out about the party, First Born was no longer considered for Fella sitting duties. However, both they and I would agree, that any of the alternatives are better than putting me into kennels. That happened twice early on in my life and was such a traumatic time that I am not ready yet to discuss it. I think I probably need counselling of some description before I can face that experience head on.

*When are they coming home????*

# CHAPTER 17

## *Obsessive Compulsive Disorder*

It was fairly early on in my life when my People thought I might either be autistic or simply have OCD. In all honesty, I think the jury is still out. What, you might ask, would make them think this? Below is a list of my little foibles, as I like to call them, which have made them categorise me thus:

1.     Routine – I have to have my routines adhered to and that includes the route we walk. If there is any digression from this I am known to pull and pant frantically in order to get back to the route. Similarly, my feeding routine needs to be kept to religiously. This is why I stare a full two hours ahead of schedule, to ensure they do not forget the routine. I must also have a dental stick in the morning (the equivalent of teeth cleaning) and a joint stick in the evening (the equivalent of a massage after my long weary day).

2.     If we are out for the day, visiting relatives, we always have to be back home by 7 p.m., 8 p.m. at the VERY latest. If we are not, I start to assume that we, or rather, I am staying and being left behind. That is when the

panting begins, the fretful pacing, the staring until my People say, 'Come on Fells, time to go home.' Once we are in the car, I am more than happy to settle down and sleep through the whole journey.

3. My bedtime routine is very important to me if I am to get a good night's shut eye. At around 7 p.m., 7.30 p.m. the very latest, I look at Mummy to convey to her that it is 'Bye-byes Time'. She, bless her, understands immediately. The telepathy is simply amazing. Off we trot, or rather I do as she opens all doors wide so that I can take a run up before I trot across the rug to the next piece of rug and into the conservatory to my bed. Sometimes I wait for her to say, 'Alley-up,' sometimes I cannot be bothered and simply dive up there, keen for my cuddle. Not that long ago, she took to saying the 'This little Piggy' rhyme and, as lovely as it was, was most unsuitable for bedtime as it got me all excited. Somehow, she came to realize this and stopped.

4. People – I'm not sure why Mummy has added this one to the list. I think it is right to be naturally cautious of strangers. I certainly remember her telling the various Minor Ones not to talk to strangers when they were younger. Being her only son, I assumed that applied to me. It seems odd therefore, that she expects me to be friendly a) when a random stranger stops us in the street to pat my head and b) when I am expected to stop barking at people who come to the door and virtually invite them in for tea! I thought I was meant to be 'on guard and in charge' – well clearly not! I let them have it with both barrels and Mummy has a Devil's own job to hold me back by the collar. I think it is important that they get the message that should they knock when They Who Must Be Obeyed are out, they will have me to contend with. As for those who stop me in the street, quite frankly, I don't know where their hands have been. Why would I want them patting my clean silky head? This is why, when they reach out to do

so, I duck my head away. My People think I am cowering when I do this. Honestly, they should know better. They do, however, get very embarrassed when I sniff the crotches of their guests. I am so sorry, but I haven't mastered the handshake yet!

5.    The weekend bones – there is an unwritten rule that, as payment for my guarding services during the week, I have a bone on a Friday night and one on a Saturday night. This also seems to coincide with them having a take away of some description. I really am not fussy what kind of bones I have, though do prefer either the bacon bone or peanut butter bones from Wolfitt's. If Mummy has had time to get into town, she always makes sure she gets these. However, when she is in a rush, which is most of the time, I have to settle for a Tesco Finest. I use 'finest' in the loosest sense of the word, as nothing could be finer than Wolffit's bones. Once, I remember (and this is why the weekend bones are listed here) Mummy forgot to get me a bone at all! I had to make do with a chew left over from my birthday which would last all of thirty seconds. I have to confess, I did make her suffer by doing my sulking stare at her for over four hours. When she tried to make it up to me with a cuddle, I turned my back on her – it absolutely broke my heart to do so, but she never made that mistake again. I have heard it said that since that day, she now keeps spare bones in the cupboard – just in case. Very wise.

6.    Noises – not just your normal noises like fireworks but any sudden noise makes me very unsettled. Mummy has spent a long time thinking back as to why that might be but cannot fathom it at all. Certainly when I was a pup in November 2004, I did wonder what the loud bangs were as we went for our final walk, though they did not bother me at that stage. I quite liked looking at the flashing lights and colours. But a couple of years later I found I liked them less and they made me jumpy. It was then I

realized that a lot of things made me jumpy: A carrier bag suddenly rustling in a hedge as I walked past, someone unlocking their car door, a bus changing gear as it goes past me, a book falling off the sofa and, the other day, a cyclist changing gear spooked me a bit. But it's other things too, like the donkeys that we pass on our half field – half lane walk. My People seem to like them but they scare the bejeezus out of me. Usually they are further in their field or standing in their little stable, but the other day, we came round the corner and they were right there, up at the fence, within feet of me. Now that did make me jump! I usually creep up closer to them and then bark, just to let them know who's boss. I did not like it when Mummy patted them on the noses. More on them later.

7.    The stairs – not just any stairs but namely the stairs at home. When I was a pup of approximately eight months old, I had made my way up stairs and was exploring the different rooms, raiding the bins, as you do. Then Mummy caught me and ordered me downstairs and for some reason unknown to man or beast, I could no longer descend the stairs. I did not know how to. I stood hovering, not sure which foot to put down first. Eventually Daddy had to pull me from the front by my collar while Mummy pushed me from behind. I went down so fast on my bottom that I got a nasty carpet burn on my bum and from that day onwards would no longer ascend the stairs. These, I have to say, are the only stairs that I am particular about. I am happy to walk upstairs in Nana and Grandad's house, Auntie Karen and Uncle Liam's house, the steep concrete steps outside our house, and at Stanam Road as well as the 80+ steps to the East Hill in Hastings.

8.    The floors – enough said on that one. I am rather alarmed, however, to hear that Benny's Mummy, Karen, has lent my Mummy a book about dog whispering, whatever that might be, in an attempt to get me to walk on

the floors. She hasn't whispered anything in my ears yet but I'll be ready and waiting when she does. Hell will have to freeze over before I walk on those shiny slippery floors!

9. Barking at thin air – or at least this is what my People think. Don't they realise that I bark for a reason. And in any case: I'm a dog – I BARK! Get over it! I have a bark for 'Beware strangers approaching who could be about to rob the house'. Then there is my 'Just to let you know friends and relations are arriving and the house should be tidy/you should have showered and dressed/applied your make-up by now bark'. These are distinct from my general 'Trying to get Mummy's attention bark so that she will feed me/get me more water/take me for my walk/ reach for my ball under the sofa/ give me a cuddle bark'. This is usually accompanied by a mournful whine and my head tilting from side to side, because of course, body language is vital to the whole communication process. But this barking at thin air business – what they don't realise is that we canines are finely tuned into the spirit world and it is these I am barking at toward them away from my family. They drift in and out, up and down and I am the only one who can sense them. I can't exactly see them, but I know they are there.

10. Finally, play time – when I go out with He and She Who Must Be Obeyed to the fields, I expect a good romp with at least one of my toys. I like to see the toy being thrown then show off my prowess as a runner tearing off to retrieve it before it has even landed on the ground. But Daddy always spoils it. He always goes for the sleight of hand – fake fetch throw – you fooled a dog! Woohoo! What a proud moment for the top of the food chain! Mummy throws it straight away as she knows I cannot bear to be teased like this. The trouble is Mummy's throws are pathetic – a Poodle could throw a ball further.

*It's such a long way up! I'll just have to lie here and wait until she comes down…*

# CHAPTER 18

## *Bad Hair Daze*

Mummy's mood is sour this morning. Now this could be for a number of reasons:

1. He Who Must be Obeyed (Sometimes) snored all night.

2. She couldn't sleep because she was thinking about school so much – she must love that place!

3. It's Wednesday – Mummy has to be in extra early because of something called 'Diaries' and despite the fact it is also 'Hump Day' (whatever that might be), she finds Wednesdays hard as she has to teach all day, oversee double assembly, and then rehearse. On Wednesdays she ends the days as sour as she begins.

4. It is a Monday – Mummy does not like Mondays – who does???

5. It is the first day back after a holiday.

"Oh Bloody hell!" – Today the reason is because, as she opens the door to take me for my morning constitution, she notices it is 'pissing down.' Slam goes the cupboard door as she hops up and down trying to get into her waterproof trousers. I love this game as her head is bent low, bobbing up and down and I take advantage and give her a lick round the chops. Having just had breakfast my breath is redolent of lamb and rice. Yum!

As we stride out, we both put our heads down as we face the wind and the rain head on. This is most unpleasant and I wonder what on earth I did wrong to warrant such an assault on my fur and feet. It's all very well if she wants to go walking in the dark at 6.45 a.m. in the pouring rain, but why does she have to drag me with her? I am going to have to figure out a way of avoiding this.

As we make our way along Canterbury Road, I remember now why we do this every day and am relieved to smell a scent where I want to cock my leg to add my own. Bliss!

Once home, I push my way first through the front door and am already waiting by the cupboard under the stairs (where my food and treats are kept) while she is trying to prise her saturated clothes off. Despite her discomfort, she never fails to towel me down and refill my water bowl.

"You're getting decidedly porky again, Fella," she says to me as she works the towel under my belly.

"Charming!" I think, "what a great start to the day this is turning out to be."

As she finishes getting ready for work, I lie down in the dining room, stretched right out to my fullest length, my nose lying along my front paws in what she has dubbed my 'Superman' pose. She hasn't quite managed to dry my snout off and now little driplets of water plop off the end of it onto the carpet. I sigh deeply and noisily. I know this is going to be a bad day. I hear the sound of Mummy's footsteps thundering down the stairs, her steps are urgent in their lateness.

"Right, you're in charge, you're on guard, stay close to Angie, don't go running off and come home safe to Mummy." This said in a monotone and at break neck speed.

What kind of farewell does she call that? As if sensing my disgust, she comes back and gives me a cuddle, recoiling slightly from my wet and steaming fur. Three kisses on the nose and then she's off.

I don't bother seeing her off from the front room window and slink off sulkily to my sofa instead. Two can play at that game.

Just before I jump up on the sofa, I look around me. There is something different about the conservatory. Uncle Liam came round recently to take all of the lights down and at the weekend, Daddy took all of the blinds down. What is going on? I'm not completely sure but I thought I heard Mummy say something about breaking up the sofa. Was she talking about my sofa? I think I had better guard that rather than anything else.

The rest of the day carries on in the same miserable vein. When Angie arrives to take me out, she looks soaked through and tired. I wag my tail at her and give her hand a lick.

"Hello Fella, come on boy," and off we go. I climb into the back of her car with three other wet and steaming doggies and off we go. Somehow, when I'm out running with the pack, it doesn't bother me if I get wet and muddy. We just love running together, looking for adventures, foraging for food.

"Oh My God! Look at the state of you!" I can see from Mummy's face that a) she is not best pleased with me and b) she is still in a sour mood.

Still in her work suit, she grabs a towel and begins the process again of drying me off. Little bit by little bit, she begins to melt and she looks at me in that soft gooey way she reserves just for me.

*I hate being wet!*

# CHAPTER 19

## *Marley And Me*

It was whilst we were taking our evening constitutional when I had my first (but no doubt not the last) altercation with the new kid on the block: Marley – how original! Mummy had the audacity to go all gooey over this ten month old black Labrador.

Before I knew it, he had his front paws on my back and his Man Parts pressed far too close for comfort against my rump. I spun round one way, which flung him in the opposite direction. Before anyone knew what was going on, we had our leads completely twisted like the ribbons in a maypole dance which had allowed our noses to be within fifty-nine millimetres of each other. My eyes were narrowed in contempt for him. His were wide and laughing as if he was mocking me.

Initially, Mummy began to laugh, laughter which then took on a nervous edge when she heard my warning growls and saw me draw my jowls back to reveal my sparkling teeth (thank you dental sticks!) Marley, in response uttered pathetic high pitched attempts at a growl.

By the time we had got our leads and legs untangled,

my hackles were raised like a Mohican. The impudence of this pup and the total lack of control his owner had over him. Odd one that, as I detected a German accent and they are usually so well organized and disciplined, the Germans. Think of their road systems (according to Daddy), their ability to bag a sun bed first (according to Mummy) and their police trained Shepherd dogs (according to me). I am not sure what hope young Marley has if he is going to have to be the lead trainer in this partnership.

As for Marley, once his owner had achieved a small degree of control over him, he continued to lean towards me, his big brown eyes so wide that they appeared to be bottomless black pools. I note, with pleasure, that Mummy mentions how much calmer I became once I'd had my Man Parts removed, so hopefully the same might happen to him. I am too harsh. But tonight I am just not in the mood to be conciliatory. I am preoccupied by the weekly changing nature of the conservatory (aka my bedroom). Perhaps, another time I will try to have a quiet word with this pup; teach him a thing or two.

As we continue our walk, Mummy asks if I want a biscuit but Dis-as-ter! There are none left in the bag. This is just not good enough and sets me into an even blacker mood.

When we get home instead of a joint stick, I get a Wolfitt Peanut Butter bone for my troubles and immediately grapple it between my paws and jaws.

"I thought you were just going round the block. You've been gone ages," Daddy complains.

"Yes, but we bumped into a gorgeous black ten month old Labrador puppy called Marley, didn't we Fells?"

I look up from my bone. "Marley? Nope, doesn't ring any bells with me." Back to the bone.

*It's all very well having a Marley but who could resist this face?*

# CHAPTER 20

## *Operation Conservatory*

Something is definitely afoot or rather apaw. I have to confess this particular operation is not going according to plan and I may have to draft in reinforcements. The evidence so far:

Week 1: Uncle Liam removes lights from the conservatory – Why? Why would he do that? Thierry has no answers for me. Now, at sunset, no one can see anything in the conservatory.

Week 2: Daddy removes the blinds from **all** of the windows. Perhaps that is to let more light in. It feels colder and more echoey in there now.

Week 3: A strange man comes in and takes the radiator away. Right under Mummy and Daddy's nose! Why would he want our radiator? Why does he not get one of his own?

So, no light, no heating, out in the freezing cold? I should cocoa! Fortunately, some fireworks began to go off and I persuaded Mummy to let me sleep in the front room on the cushions on the leather sofa – bliss!

DISASTER! It has happened. Whilst I was not looking,

my bed, my beloved sofa has been taken! Vanished! Gone!
Who could have done such a dastardly thing? And, to
make matters worse, Mummy seems to think that I can
make do with my old basket that has suddenly appeared
from the loft. All of this weekend, they have both been
moving every bit of furniture out of the conservatory and
putting it into the dining room, making an already small
room, tiny and cramped. Then, most strangely, they laid
out two huge pieces of blue material across the floor of the
conservatory. It is not slippery and makes a sort of crackly
noise when I walk on it. I think I heard Mummy call it Tar-
Paul-In. No idea what that is or what it is for. I am
beginning to think that they are going to turn the
conservatory into a swimming pool, except it would not be
deep enough for humans so maybe it's going to be a doggy
pool for me! How lovely, but a bit excessive.

Whatever it is going to be I think it was supposed to
happen today, the first day of the half term holidays. I heard
Mummy make a phone call asking what time the workmen
were going to arrive. Whatever the person on the other end
said, made Mummy's face go white, then very red, and then
she said a very naughty word. Then she started shouting,
which isn't like Mummy, unless the children have made her
very cross or I have done annoying habit no. 1. Apparently,
there has been a 'monumental cock-up' she was relating to
Daddy on the phone. He was definitely angry as I could
hear his voice from several feet away. So now my swimming
pool has been delayed for another two weeks! I still haven't
been able to work out if it will have a floating bed area and
one of those nifty swim up bars where I can eat and drink to
my heart's content. My pals in the Pembury Crew will be so
jealous – will have to see if Mummy will let me invite them
over for a pool party.

Watch this space!

OK Doggy Pool update: Very early this weekend, four
strange men arrived and began attacking the conservatory

— literally, taking it down bit by bit. The gardens, back and front look a real mess with pieces of the old conservatory stacked parallel with what looks like pieces of a new conservatory. So no doggy swimming pool for me! However, there is still something not quite right. I heard Mummy go mad again when she discovered two crucial bits of the structure were missing.

Nevertheless, the tea drinking men are continuing with their work and Mummy, Daddy and I are confined mostly to the front room.

Day 3 of the Conservatory saga: We now have a brand new conservatory. It is clean, white and huge. Unlike the last one, this one does not seem to turn into a sauna if it's sunny or a freezer if it is cold outside. I have had a new bed bought for me with something called a memory foam mattress. It is not exactly like my last bed, a two seater sofa, but nonetheless, it will have to make do for now.

*Not exactly a three seater sofa, but it will have to do!*

# CHAPTER 21

## *A Year On*

It has been six months since I last added to my memoirs and so much has happened. Although day to day life at Chez Wade continues as normal, in the past six months Mummy has got a new job which she begins very soon. Her new title, Vice Principal, sounds rather grand. She says it will mean longer hours. I am not quite sure this is possible as, apart from her normal 7.30 a.m. – 7 p.m. hours, she often works throughout the night. I must keep my eye on her and make sure she has lots of cuddles and licks. The name of her new school Bonus Pastor sounds rather intriguing and delicious. Bone Us Pasta – sounds like food is involved – will keep my nose to the ground.

We are currently on six weeks holiday and it's been an interesting one. Despite their vehement promises never to allow First Born to dog-sit me again, they swanned off with the other three teenagers to somewhere hot and involving an aeroplane and left me to fend for myself with aforementioned First Born. To be fair she was out working a lot of the time and Angie came in to walk me. Nor were there any 'parttttyyyyyys' as such, just four of her female friends round for a pizza, movie and some strange coloured liquids. Much to my disgust there wasn't a great deal of bosom nuzzling allowed this time; something to do with my moulting fur and making their chests as hairy as a badger's bottom!

I think we are now in our third week of the holidays and so far Mummy has yet to take me to Rockanore or meet up with Benny and Buddy. It really isn't the standard of holiday day care that I have come to know and love. In fact I have noticed she's spending rather a lot of time on her lap top on something called 'Facebook'. She appears to be creating photo albums, some of them are of me and I feel like saying, 'But I'm here! It's me! Spend time with me, not that silly old lap top!' But I know it's no use when I see that her eyes are glazed over. Sometimes, they are all on their lap tops, in the same room 'talking' to each other, but not saying a word or even looking at each other! How can that be? Humans are very strange…

Today, 12 August 2012 has been a very special day indeed. I am so pleased my birthday falls in the summer holidays as Mummy can always be with me to celebrate. I began the day with my usual bowlful of food but then followed by lots of presents of assorted shapes and sizes wrapped up in green wrapping paper with footballs on it. Suitably boyish, I thought. My birthday card says '8 today – Happy 8th birthday' but I am not as interested in that as I am the presents. My keen sense of smell tells me there are some edible ones amongst them and, sure enough, there is a large bag of pick 'n' mix dog biscuits and two bones from Wolfitt's: Peanut Butter and Bacon – I am drooling already. These are accompanied by a new rubber ball and a new blanket for my bed.

I am so thrilled that I run around with the ball in my mouth (still with wrapping paper on) for several minutes before Mummy can wrestle me to the ground. I am even more excited by the new blanket and try to take it with me on my morning walk, but Mummy insists I leave it at the door as she says it makes me look like a needy child – I am a needy child! We compromise and I leave it on the door step though instantly regret this as I realize that anyone from next door's cat to the postman could come and steal it.

Mid-morning, Mummy takes me and two of the teenagers (used to be the Sensible One and the Mad One but are now just run of the mill teenagers) to Haysden Country Park. This seems to be my annual birthday treat. Last year, Mummy managed to lose my birthday Frisbee when she accidently flung it high up into some bushes. This year she has brought my new ball along, so I'd better keep a close eye on that.

Things were going swimmingly well. There is so much to sniff and smell (aside from other dogs' bottoms) at Haysden and there's also the lake! Mummy doesn't like me going into the lake as she says it makes me smell like a sewerage works, whatever that is. I was determined to have a dip one way or another, but I didn't bargain on nearly drowning!

One minute we were walking along a path in the forest, then I dived off to the left to investigate a particularly pungent smell. Before I knew it, I had come to the edge of a bank, couldn't stop in time and went straight over the edge into a wide and deep river. Within seconds I could hear Mummy's voice calling, initially in her normal tone, then higher pitched with an edge of panic to it.

"Come and get a biscuit!" I really wanted to. Oh how I wanted that biscuit, but I couldn't scramble up the bank to get back out. I had managed to wedge my front legs up onto the ledge of the bank, but my back legs were scrambling furiously, like mini-propellers in the water, but finding nothing to grip onto. I am sure it was only seconds, but it felt like minutes before I finally saw Mummy push her way through the undergrowth.

As her eyes met mine, she could see the panic in my

face. My eyes, normally relaxed brown pools of chocolate, were wide, black and frightened. My jaw was slightly open, my teeth gritted in determination to get out. There was a split second of panic in her eyes as I could tell she was wondering how on earth she was going to get me out. Then she lurched forward, hooked her right hand through my collar and pulled as hard as she could.

"Come on Boy!"

Somehow, with her pulling and her encouraging words, it gave me the impetus I needed to push with my back legs as hard as I could and I was suddenly launched out of the water like a black bullet. I ran straight past Mummy, up the slope through the undergrowth, soaking her as I went.

Oh, she went through the motions of sounding cross, calling me 'stupid' (quite hurtful on my birthday) but she couldn't stay angry for long. Both relieved I was back on dry land, we'd have loved to have had a celebratory cuddle but it wasn't to be as I now smelt like a sewer.

The rest of the walk went without further incident, apart from when a young male black Labrador called Alfie chased me into the lake. I was trying to run away from him but he forced me in there! We had a good swim, such fun! By now, Mummy had given up on all hopes of me remaining dry during this walk and was resigned to having to bath me when we got home. Nor did it stop her treating me to a birthday ice cream, which of course, I demolished within twenty seconds. I still don't know why I never get to have the chocolate flake. It's not as though I really need to watch my weight, although I heard Mummy say that particular ship has sailed – Cheek!

*Recovering after my near drowning at Haysden Country Park.*

*Happiness is: A dog and his ice cream!*

Later on that afternoon while we were all sat quietly in the lounge watching television, the lights suddenly went out and Mummy came in holding a bowl with a sausage in it. The sausage was glowing in the light of eight candles. I was serenaded by all, even Daddy who looked a tad embarrassed, before Mummy blew out the candles while I made my wish: More food, of course!

# CHAPTER 22

## *Update On All Annoying Habits*

I am very proud to announce that many of the aforementioned habits my People find annoying have been eliminated. I don't know whether this is due to my emerging maturity or simply because I disgust myself sometimes.

I no longer eat poo, hump my bed or rip up my bedding. I do, unfortunately still drool, stare, fart, wake them up early, shed my hair everywhere, lick Mummy's face and bark at thin air. Still three out of ten isn't bad.

As for their annoying habits, I have managed to wear them down on quite a few:

I no longer wear an Arsenal collar or eat from an Arsenal bowl – it's interesting but over the past two years as Arsene Wenger has refused to buy in more defenders, so the Arsenal memorabilia has been removed.

I get to sleep up on the leather sofa, supposedly with the soft cushions covering the leather, but frequently, I just get up, cushions or not. Occasionally, like tonight, Daddy catches me up there, but he can't stay cross with me for long when he looks into my big brown eyes and sees my tail wagging softly. If I open my mouth a little, it looks as if I'm smiling, and then he melts completely.

They rarely keep me waiting for my food or walk these days. I have perfected the stare to the extent that they have to see to my every need, just to stop my eyes boring through their heads into their brains.

Otherwise, unfortunately, they still have all the remaining annoying habits all seven of them! That's not very good. In fact some of their annoying habits have worsened over the past few months. For example:

Calling me a scaredy cat. This has become quite intolerable, helped by the fact that all the local cats are feisty to the point of being terrifying. The Siamese halfway up Canterbury Road stared me out the other day, and when I lurched towards it, with my puffiest chest, it lurched back towards me! I jumped back into Mummy's legs which meant I couldn't get as far away from it as I'd have liked. A quick side step saved the day and I trotted on as if nothing had happened; I am plotting my revenge, nonetheless.

Then there is the tortoiseshell in Sandhurst Road. Now this one needs a right royal slap. It sits, nay lies right in the middle of the pavement and, as I approach, it doesn't do that usual cat thing of rising up to look as tall as possible, spitting at me. Oh no, it spreads its bulk out as far as possible to occupy as much space as possible so that I have no alternative but to go up on the grass bank AROUND it!

All of these occasions combine to have me declared a scaredy cat of the scarediest order.

There is a new annoying habit that we both share: I call it The Biscuit Conundrum but Mummy shortens this title to The Biscuit Con.

From my point of view, the writing on the side of the biscuit box clearly states that a dog of my size should be having 6-8 biscuits a day. Now, apart from my bowl of food at breakfast, my pre morning walk biscuit, my half dental stick, my pre and post afternoon walk biscuit (which obviously I do not get when being walked by Angie), my bowl of food at dinner time, my pre last walk of the day biscuit and half a joint stick, I calculate that I am currently at least 2-6 biscuits a day short of the recommended daily intake. So I have started expecting biscuits at other junctures, for example:

·   When I say hello nicely to another dog.

·   When I have been frightened by a bus or other large and noisy vehicle whooshing past.

·   When we see the donkeys – even if they have already been put to bed.

·   When I retrieve my new birthday ball when Mummy has thrown it across the field – three times.

So, roughly speaking, on an average day that would bring me somewhere closer to solving the Biscuit Conundrum.

Mummy, on the other hand, simply thinks all this expecting a biscuit 'for the least little thing' has become a Biscuit Con and has got far too out of hand. The other day, she took one look at my belly and has nicknamed me The Biscuit Barrel – Cheek!

*How chilled out am I? Does my bum look big in this photo??*

# CHAPTER 23

## *Remember, Remember The 5th November*

Oh my DOG! Every year it's the same! 5th November –
Firework night. Except it's never just the 5th is it? This year
it's the 4th, 5th, 6th and 12th for Heaven's sake! All because
the 'organisers' of fireworks displays at Dunorlan Park,
Pembury Village Green and the King William the VI pub
do not want to clash: Never a thought for canine or feline
feelings.

This year Mummy went to the vet to get me some
doggy Valium. She must love me very much to go to such
lengths to stop me from suffering. Either that or she's fed
up of spending another firework season with me under the
dining room table, her small arms outstretched around my
cowering shaking body, her face trying to avoid my hot
dog's dinner breath.

Whatever the reason, Calmex was supposed to do just
that. When she held the tablets out to me, I was very
sneaky; I turned my nose up at them and walked away. As
I did so, I heard the predictable heavy sigh as, with heavier

steps she made her way to the cupboard under the stairs where my food is kept. She dug the cup into the bag of food, popped the two tablets inside, then nonchalantly tossed the food into my bowl, trying to convince me it only contained dog food. Greedily and gratefully, I wolfed the food down, Calmex and all.

Mummy was pleased with me and I began to hope that I would need Calmex every night. About an hour after I had taken it, I started to feel my legs turn to jelly and my eyelids got heavier. Soon I was fast asleep on the sofa, oblivious to the distant bangs of squibs. This method of coping was going well until the King William fireworks began. The King William as the crow flies is approximately ten yards from my back garden. Admittedly the fireworks only lasted ten minutes, but I heard Daddy say they were of such an industrial strength that it sounded like we were in the middle of a war zone – and there we were back under the dining room table, Mummy's arms around me, me shaking vigorously and panting heavily in her face.

So, the campaign to ban fireworks begins – or at least that's what Mummy said. I haven't seen any posters or petitions though, she hasn't been to any meetings. I think she's forgotten my palpable fear, she can no longer remember the smell of panic emanating from my doggy chops, nor the thunderous beating of my petrified heart. It is no longer of any concern to her that every time I hear a firework I feel as though my world is crashing down around my soft black velvet ears. She can be fickle. I suppose on the plus side it means I get an extra cupful of food and extra cuddles every time these things go off.

The picture below is my 'Where's the Calmex? I hear thunder/fireworks and I need it now! – face.'

# CHAPTER 24

## *Fella In Love - Valentine's Day*

Every year on 14 February He and She Who Must Be Obeyed exchange cards and presents. Mummy even buys me a card in which she writes things like: To my darling Fella, Happy Valentine's Day with all my love Mummy. This was followed by lots of kisses. Sweet! One year she also bought me a present, a bright red heart shaped food bowl. It's a bit effeminate but as long as my food is in it and it hasn't got the Arsenal logo plastered all around it, what do I care?

The main reason I include this chapter is because of a remark made by the Mad One the other day where she declared that dogs could not fall in love. What nonsense! Dogs are capable of feeling many different feelings. Sometimes I feel sad (when I'm missing my People), sometimes I feel scared (when a member of the Pembury Massive squares up to me when I'm out on my daily walk with Angie and Daddy is not around to defend me with his special metal bat), sometimes I feel happy (mainly when I am with Mummy and Daddy, or food is about to arrive). But I have felt the pangs of true love, oh yes!

She was a cheeky little filly – a Cocker Spaniel – I always get on best with Spaniels. Her name was Posy and she had beautiful brown soulful eyes that used to snatch quick glances at me before turning away and trotting off, her derriere swaying provocatively. I would then trot after her, my head held high, my gait firm and strong. Having caught up with her, I used to drop my head down to hers. She would look up at me and our noses would touch, sniffing gently. It was pretty much love at first sight. She had become a part of the Pembury Crew but only walked with Angie on Tuesdays and Thursdays, so I had to make the most of my time with her.

I knew it was love because a) When I didn't see her on Mondays, Wednesdays and Fridays I felt a certain emptiness in my chest and b) I began to notice one day that Beastiewinks, a German Shepherd, also a new addition to the Pembury Crew had begun to make doggy eyes at my Posy. Blooming cheek! Ever a polite girl, she did not like to be rude to him but I could tell she did not relish his attention. Whenever I saw him trying to get into her good books, I felt a strange hot feeling rising in my chest. It used to burn there all the way up to my eyes which bore into the back of Beastiewinks's head willing it to explode on the spot. As my hackles rose and my eyes narrowed, I overheard Angie saying, "I think Fella is feeling jealous!" So that was what the feeling was called – jealousy. Yes, I recognised the signs in Daddy when I licked my Man Parts. He used to stare at me with a look that could kill.

I tried to think of ways to win Posy over. I was fairly sure she liked me but I used to get so tongue tied when we were together. My paws became sweaty, I had palpitations in my chest, and my mouth, usually moist, was bone dry. I kept thinking of the films I'd watched with the Mad Ones: 101 Dalmatians, The Lady and The Tramp. Classic tales of doggy love. But how was I going to take Posy out to an Italian restaurant? How could I engineer it for her to come and live with me? No, it was no good, I would have to settle for Tuesdays and Thursdays and sharing her with that German fiend.

As luck would have it, I needn't have worried. Six months after moving to Pembury, Posy's family were moving on again. It had only been a temporary stay while her Daddy found a new job. She was going to be moving to somewhere called Chipping Norton and we were to be parted. Forever. Never to see one another again. I was devastated. I had already begun rehearsing the name Posy Wade in my head, imagined us trotting side by side. We could never of course have had puppies, thanks to my People having my Man Parts chopped off, but I think we could have weathered that one. She was quite an independent girl who did not feel that motherhood was her only destiny.

The day we parted was, to date, one of the saddest days of my life. We walked our usual route together, side by side. By now Beastiewinks had given up and done the noble thing and stood aside – a definite show of pedigree breeding. Posy promised she would never forget me and I promised that if my People were ever to journey with me to Chipping Norton, I would make every attempt to look her up. Just before I jumped out of Angie's car, Posy and I pressed noses one last time. Forlornly, I walked slowly up the steps to my house, walked through the door that Angie had opened for me and lay quietly on the floor in the dining room. I tried to be manly about it but I couldn't stop the single tear roll down my fur onto the carpet.

That night Mummy noticed I was very quiet and although I still ate my dinner (nothing puts me off my food), she could tell I was not my usual self. "Do you think he's coming down with something?" she asked Daddy.

"He's fine," he replied.

But what did he know? Men, human men, do not seem

to experience the pangs and pains of true love. In the human world, I would clearly be regarded as New Man with all my empathetic qualities and romantic tendencies. In the meantime, I had to nurse my broken heart with only Mummy for comfort. She tried her best but as she did not know the reason for my sadness, she could not offer me any of the usual platitudes such as, 'Plenty more pups in the field'. But I was grateful for her comforting arms and I knew somehow, she intuitively knew that I was going through a difficult time in my life.

*My beloved Posy – February 2011.*

# CHAPTER 25

## *George And Mojo*

For those of you who have been paying attention, you may recall back in chapters seventeen and twenty-two respectively, I mentioned two donkeys that I was not particularly fond of. Well, as with all things in my life, my relationship with them has moved on. I am no longer terrified of these poor creatures. Indeed, I positively look forward to the times when my People say, "Shall we go and see George and MoJo?" for that is their names. In fact, my instinct for reading Mummy's mind is now so sharp, that I know if she goes to the kitchen and begins to cut some apples or carrots, then it's 'George and MoJo time'!

Now please do not be mistaken into thinking that as I am moving towards my senior years, I am maturing and extending the proverbial olive branch of friendship to my equine acquaintances. Oh no! It is not this at all! It is, in fact, my latest attempt to solve the Biscuit Conundrum (Chapter twenty-two – Do keep up!)

Once these smelly, hairy, bad-tempered creatures have been fed and (annoyingly) petted by She Who Must Be Obeyed, then she turns to me and gives me 4-5 little biscuits. That is the reason why I enjoy going to see George and MoJo. Just recently, we have taken to sniffing each other's noses between the wooden bars of the fence that separates us. That is about as close as I would like to get as I have seen that MoJo can be a bit handy with his hooves and poor George has been given a hefty kick in the behind to get him out of the way of any food opportunities.

I must confess, I am none too pleased by the amount of attention Mummy and Daddy give them. They tickle them behind their ears and under their chins, pat their cheeks and speak to them in warm cooing tones, the way they do me. Nonetheless, they remain firmly behind that side of the fence whilst we walk back up the lane. Together! Me with a smug look on my face.

*My snack buddies George and MoJo (George is the shifty looking one in the foreground).*

# CHAPTER 26

## *On The Move Again*

Just when I thought we were Home Sweet Home, Happy Ever After, the board went up – For Sale through Barnes Kingsnorth. It is a different coloured board from last time so I am hoping that the people are nicer. I am not too pleased to be on the move again. When the lady came to take photos of my home, I tried to delay the whole process by sitting in each and every shot. The lady, who has a Retriever and a Spaniel herself, simply laughed and said something about it helping the house to sell even more quickly if I was in all of the photos.

I am not sure exactly where our new home will be but Mummy and Daddy have mentioned places such as Bromley and, more excitingly, Petts Wood. Now this place sounds amazing! A whole wood just for pets! Well that's a bit of me. There are a few things I'm a bit concerned about though:

1.  What if all the floors are shiny?

2.  What if the locals are feral?

3.  What if I get lost while out walking?

4.    Who is going to walk me during the day – I'm not sure Angie will come as far as Bromley…

5.    Where will I sleep?

I am sure there will be more concerns when I have thought of them.

*\*\*\**

Latest news is that my home has now been sold but the worrying news is that we have yet to find a new home. Mummy seems very tense at the moment even though it's the summer holidays when she is usually more relaxed than at any time of the year. I think it is all to do with the moving house business. She and Daddy spend most weekends looking for houses, which I think is very odd. There are lots of houses around. You don't have to look for them, just open your eyes and there they are!

Just when I was looking forward to spending lots of time going on lovely summer holiday walks, Mummy announces yet again that I must be on guard and in charge while she goes 'HOUSE HUNTING'. I mean, how do you hunt down a house? Do you track it down and… then what – shoot it? Is that how you get a house?

One day towards the end of the summer holidays, Mummy, Daddy and I went on a long journey in the car. I had no idea where we were going but they seemed pretty excited. After six ten minutes snoozes, the car eventually stopped in a road I had never seen before in my life. I jumped out of the car cautiously, sniffing the air voraciously. Nope – definitely not been here before.

"Come on Fells," Daddy called, for it was he who had the lead, Mummy being armed with the poop scooper. We walked back up the road, away from the car and then seemed to stop outside a particular house. I had a good sniff at the driveway and the little low wall in the front garden. Unusually for my People, they did not try to drag me away, but let me continue to sniff to my heart's content. Eventually, I left my usual calling card and trotted on my way, fairly confident we would be back this way again.

It seemed like a nice road, it seemed like a generally nice area. We went for quite a long walk around more roads I had never trodden on before, eventually ending up on something called the High Street. I was not as keen on the High Street. There were lots of people not looking where they were going. There were cars and buses whooshing past me, changing gear and making that noise that makes me cower down. Eventually, we turned off this manic road and began walking back along a road I now remembered. I could smell my scent and started to sniff my way back to the car.

About seven minutes later, I stopped outside a house. I sniffed the ground, I put my nose in the air and sniffed the air. My eyes glanced over the building in front of me. Yes, this is where I had stopped earlier. And then, something odd happened. Daddy let me walk up to the front door and give it an almighty sniff. I wonder if this is to be my new home. Is this the hearth over which I am to defend to my death? I looked at my People expectantly. Their eyes were shining with excitement. Yes, I do believe they have brought me to see the new house. How very thoughtful of them. They must love me very much. The big question though, was when was it all going to happen?

I need not have wondered that for long. By the time Mummy was five weeks back at school, so the boxes began to appear. To be fair, I was not much alarmed by this as my People had started leaving the odd empty box lying around for me to get used to. By early October, however, the house, room by room, was filled with packed boxes from floor to ceiling. Where did all this stuff come from? The loft by the looks of it. It was organised chaos and I did start to feel a little nervous at this point. Nervous that I would not be able to find my food bowl, my bed, my way out of the front door but most of all that I'd be left behind and not make it to the new house at all. Suppose they lost sight of me amongst all the boxes and managed to leave without me? Supposing those photos of this house did have me appearing in them after all and the new owners insisted I came with the property!

This theory grew stronger before we moved when they decided to give me a shower upstairs in their bathroom. Now I hadn't been upstairs for seven years since I was a little pup. They had bought me a special rubber mat to put in the bath so that I didn't slip and slide around. Daddy carried me upstairs like a shepherd carrying a sheep. The water was lovely and warm, not like the freezing cold stuff they get out of the water butt. And clean, the water was so clean. It is incredible how much dirt can come out of a doggy coat when it's washed with warm clean water. Afterwards I got the chance to run around upstairs and got a brief glimpse of the room – Mummy's and Daddy's room – where I first slept as a pup and new member of the family. I remembered the tiny basket with the dog paw print pattern placed next to Mummy's side of the bed that I had slept in. I remembered the little clock she put in the bed next to me and the way she used to tickle my belly to help me get to sleep. Ah happy days. Before they knew it I had sauntered downstairs, happy with my lot, but not before I heard Daddy muttering, "Why the bloody hell can't he walk UP the stairs?"

*There were boxes everywhere you looked!*

# CHAPTER 27

## *Home Is Where The Heart Is*

On the day of the move itself, completely unannounced, three burly men with a massive lorry arrived at the house. If they'd come to rob us, I would have had to say, 'Help yourself, my good men,' as I could not have taken them all on, even with Daddy and his blue bat. I need not have worried, however, as Daddy greeted them by rolling his eyes which he does a lot these days and Mummy yelled something about my lead. Before I knew it lead and collar were attached and she was leading me out of the house. At that moment, as Mummy shut the door behind us both, she looked down at me and I looked up at her and realised the door was shut on my first home and I would never see it again. I gulped deeply and followed Mummy down the steps. We appeared to be going for a walk but halfway down the road, Angie was driving towards us. When she saw us she stopped. I was expecting an emotional and tearful goodbye but instead I was ushered into the back of Angie's car, the boot shut and off we went. I looked out of the back window at Mummy as we drove off, unable to believe what had just happened. So was this it then? Were they moving without me and I was going to live with Angie?

My heart plummeted like a lift out of control as I reflected upon my situation. All day we were walking and with each new pick up of dogs, it just confirmed to me that, indeed, I was not going back home and it did look like my new home was with Angie. I loved Angie, but she was not my Mummy or Daddy. I couldn't believe that they would have made this choice and wracked my brains as to why this had been their course of action. Was it financial? Was I now too expensive to keep? Did they think I wouldn't get used to a new home in a new area? In which case, why take me all the way to see the blessed house – that was cruel.

At some point well after my tea time, I was still cogitating this tragic turn of events in my life, when I thought I heard a familiar sound. I turned and sniffed the air. If I wasn't much mistaken, I could smell Mummy. Facing the gate, I saw her pop her head over and wave at me. She had come for me after all! It is hard to describe how ecstatic I was but it was like all my birthdays, Christmases and bones had come at once. We all stood on the pavement, me with my head on my food bowl having a good scoff while Mummy and Angie were saying good bye to one another, getting a bit teary-eyed. After a last huge hug and a kiss from Angie I climbed into the back of the car with the teenager (sometimes known as the Mad One) and off we went to our new home and our new life together.

As the car pulled up to the new house, I jumped out and bounded towards the front door before putting on the emergency brakes – WOODEN FLOORS!!!! No!!!!! There were no rugs down and Daddy appeared to be fighting with a sofa. I walked around outside with the teenager while Mummy frantically got some rugs down. At last I was able to run into my new home. I ran straight out into the garden – grass again! It was bliss sniffing around and leaving my scent. Before long, I ran inside and ran upstairs. The stairs in this house were all carpeted and easy to climb and there were two flights right up to the top where Mummy and Daddy were to sleep.

The first night was very exciting, especially being able to go upstairs and be with Mummy and Daddy whenever I wanted. Mummy, however, said I needed to get used to sleeping downstairs on my sofa and, exhausted by the intense emotions of the day, I soon fell into a deep and contented sleep.

Daddy was to spend two days at home with me, unpacking and getting me used to the house and area. Although I was living in a completely new place, I felt happy as I had all of my things around me, Mummy and Daddy kept to my routines and of course, I had them. The following week was half term week and Mummy and the Teenager were home all week with me, so we were able to spend some time exploring the local area.

Although we are officially in London, it is surprising how many parks and woods there are nearby. In the first few days we noticed as we walked around the local streets that there were very few dogs, absolutely no Labradors at all and people generally did not smile at us. But as time passed and we found more doggy focused places to walk, so we found more doggies and doggy friendly people. Compared to the Pembury Massive, the dogs here appear to be really friendly and not gang affiliated at all. I have heard though, that if you cross the border into Croydon, they are a different breed over there – all Pit-bulls and Mastiffs. Daddy still does not take any chances and carries the blue bat with us when we go to the fields.

Once Mummy went back to work, then life was a little different. Daddy generally takes me for a thirty minute walk in the morning around seven and then that is it until somebody comes home. Usually it's Daddy around 2 p.m., but if not, Mummy rushes back from work in a bit of a lather as she has fifty minutes to drive home, short walk me and drive back without being missed. So there is never any time for niceties. Although I do need to go out during the day, it is hard when Mummy rushes off again and I know that is it for another five hours or so.

I have taken to commandeering the red cuddler chair in the front room. It has become my look out post although more often than not, I slump down and fall fast asleep. I am quite pleased about this as it was resolution number 7 on my 2012 New Year's Resolution list.

So the first eight years of my life I was a country dog living in a village. I now look forward to the next (hopefully) eight years being a 'city' dog living in a town.

*Another chair claimed!*

# CHAPTER 28

## *The Wonderful World Of West Wickham*

It has been nine whole months since we moved to the mean streets of London. The name's still Wade – Fella Wade but instead of keeping my eyes peeled for gangs of rampaging rabbits, I'm always on the lookout for knife-wielding Rottweilers. I have to say though, so far, the genial Labrador is in the ascendancy around this neck of the woods. (I really must stop using such quaint country expressions now that I am a City Boy).

Life is different in that I no longer run with the pack and occasionally, around lunch time, I wonder what they are doing and where they are running without me. Most days Daddy comes home to walk me or if he is away, Mummy comes racing back from work, runs in, grabs my scooper and lead and we're off at break neck speed around the block. No time for sniffing another chap's urine or any other niceties. Nope, I have to cock and squat as quickly as possible before we're back through the front door again and she's off, back to work. At which point I while away the next few hours until somebody is able to come home and feed me.

We had a long winter but the house was snuggly warm, unlike our Pembury House. I have a number of places where I can bed down for the night: the cuddler chair by the window in the front room (in case of late night guarding duties) the sofa in the back room (historically this has always been my bed) the cuddler chair next to it (not sure what happened there – think I staggered onto it by accident and then it was a done deal) and of course my memory foam bed which is upstairs in Mummy and Daddy's room.

Now that it is summer, it is lovely to have a proper garden again with grass to lie on and munch. But this summer, 2013, the heat has been too too much for one such as me. If I move I moult, if I don't move Mummy comes along and starts pulling out plugs of fur that are hanging off me. Every day she brushes me taking off five or more brush loads of hair. A whole new Labrador could have been created with the amount I have lost. And have I shed any weight? Of course not! Life just doesn't seem to work like that.

I am nearly nine now with plenty of white hairs on my chin and an achiness in my bones when I stand up and stretch. I also have a new vet now that we have moved. The surgery is called 'Tender Paws' which I think is a complete misnomer. As soon as you walk through the door your paws are assaulted by a tile floor. How am I supposed to walk on that? On my first visit the vet had to come into the waiting room to do the consult because I refused to move off the (also inappropriately named) 'Welcome' mat. He warned Mummy it couldn't happen again and next time I would simply have to walk on the floor. Mummy tried to explain that I did not walk on anything other than carpets or rugs and he gave her such a withering look that if I could have reached him I would have been tempted to nip his ankles.

On my next visit to the vet, Mummy insisted that Daddy came along as she knew what would have to happen. When the time came Daddy went through the charade of trying to persuade me to walk across the floor to the practice room. I dug my claws into the mat and pulled in the opposite direction on my lead wincing and grinding my teeth with the effort. Our eyes met and he knew it was no good. He knelt down beside me, scooped his arms around my body and lifted me shepherd style towards the vet's room. The vet on duty rolled her eyes, the other occupants of the waiting room sniggered and Mummy put her head down and shuffled along quickly behind us. I have rarely been so embarrassed, but I can't help it! I want to do it but I'm terrified! Fortunately for all of us there was a door leading out from the practice room to the back of the surgery straight into the car park. That's the door I'm using next time.

The walks I go on now are: long block walk which involves walking all the way up Copse Avenue, past the woods and back down towards home again, medium block and short block – both pretty boring but my favourites are to walk through the woods and onto the rugby fields or to walk over to the West Wickham playing fields where I get to chase my blue ball. The only downside to this venue is the amount of dogs who want to mount me. I'm not into all that sort of nonsense of domination so I just run away. Trouble is at nearly nine there is only so long I can keep running for and if they are persistent, they get me anyway. Daddy got furious with one dog which wouldn't leave me alone and I thought he was finally going to put the blue rounders bat to use.

So far we have had our first Christmas here and I am about to have my first birthday here. Normally Mummy takes me out for the morning to a local park. It used to be Haysden but I think that might be too far away now. I hope she takes me to Crystal Palace Park. We've been there before. I thought it sounded suitably royal for me but I could not see any palace while I was there and certainly not one made of crystal. Nonetheless, they have a doggy swimming lake and that's all a hound wants on a hot day – and an ice cream of course.

*GUESS WHO???????*

# CHAPTER 29

## *Social Networking*

At my grand old age of nearly nine, I have acquired a Facebook account (or as I like to call it a 'Facebark' account. It took some doing as initially those nerdy geeks at Facebook did not believe I was not human! They would not accept my name of Fella as they felt it was a nickname. I did think I should have used Lyons Range Happy Harrison but that would take far too long to type in each time I logged on. Then I remembered what Angie used to call me 'Fellsby' and that did the trick. Those 'super intelligent' chinless wonders at Facebook didn't twig at all, even with my handsome profile photo. Within the first hour I had acquired dozens of new friends. Thierry was on there (he kept that secret) and it's a great way to keep in touch with friends I don't see any more. I have tried looking for Posy but clearly her People do not let her have an account.

I have added photo albums, books and films I like, including '101 Dalmatians', music that I like, including Bob Marley so if you look me up you'll see I have many friends.

Mummy said I could have my own account as long as I

accepted her as a friend so she could keep an eye on what I was up to – cheek! So far I have made lots of albums of my handsome self which all my friends have clicked 'like' to. And when I go to new places, I can post those on too and comment on their dog friendly qualities. Other than that, I do not get to network much. There are some nice dogs here in West Wickham. Two, in particular, Nancy the Spaniel and Saffron the Setter, are rather charming ladies who prefer the gentle dog rather than the rough and ready hound. When we meet we tend to greet by sniffing noses rather than the other end. I think they are probably too elderly to have Facebook accounts; I certainly haven't found them on there.

Unfortunately, rather a large number of cats reside around my home. There are two next door – a ginger cat and one that resembles a large cotton wool ball with dirty grey smears all over it. Both are partial to coming into my garden and doing their business. Now that Mummy and Daddy have been renovating the garden and putting in new plants, the last thing they want is to see the signs of cats digging and piles of steam and stench. There is also a black cat two doors down and several tabbies further up the road or across the road. All seem to think my garden is fair game, so my key duty these days is to guard the garden against the cats. Now, during the holidays when my people are here and the back garden door is open, this is quite a simple process. I lie very still on the sofa in the back room and the first sight of a whisker or a claw on my territory and I leap up like a salmon and barrelling down the garden with my teeth bared, growl and bark at them. So far none of them have tried to stare me down – I am not sure what I would do if they did. For I have heard cats are cunning creatures and spiteful with it and I wouldn't want my beautiful handsome face scarred for life.

I don't think I'll be adding any cats to my friend list – I'd have to be barking mad!

*Me in my favourite place – my garden, looking out for cats! Why I think they are in the sky I do not know – but as Daddy always says, "You can't be too careful!"*

# CHAPTER 30

## *Turning Nine*

"I cannot believe you are nine years old Fella!" Mummy's voice sounded incredulous and to be honest, I can't believe it either. I had lots of cards and presents to open this morning, a lovely one from Nana and Grandad that Nana had customised just for me with a gold 9 and a gold F on the front. Thierry and his People sent a lovely card through about how fun it was being nine as well as some rather delicious low fat treats (not sure what he is trying to tell me there). But Mummy and Daddy's card was the best about how cool and fun I was being their nine year old son! And there was a birthday badge with a 9 on for me to wear on my collar!

Most of my presents seem to be food based this year. It is, I admit, difficult to know what to get for a dog who has everything and wants for nothing. I really do not need any more blankets or toys, so food treats like gravy bones are extremely acceptable.

My birthday outing this year was to Crystal Palace Park. Even Daddy, who was supposed to be working, came with us. The dogs at Crystal Palace really are a different breed, so polite, so well-mannered and they come when they are called. There really is no need for the blue metal bat, but Daddy says, "You can never be too careful." I have never fully understood that expression – you're either careful, or you're not. Anyway, the dogs are a delight, though I still have not made any real friends in the nearly year that I have resided in this area. I think that is the difference between city living and country life. Everyone seems busier, places to go, lamp posts to sniff, deals to be done. There's just no time to sniff noses and run together in the wind or play chase.

Having said that, I think I am getting a little too old for all that caper. I have noticed that I can only run for the ball and fetch a total of four times before I'm completely knackered. In fact sometimes I run for it but am far too puffed out to bring it back. "I thought you were supposed to be a retriever!" I hear my Daddy cruelly mock as my sides are puffed out and panting like a puff adder.

I feel like yelling back, "Yeah, well when you are the age of sixty-three (which is my equivalent age in human years), let's see how far and fast you can run for the ball!" Of course, I say nothing but turn my back on him in my best show of contempt.

Mummy has noticed I am getting older and I notice that she has noticed. She doesn't say anything, just stares into my eyes, nods her head ever so slightly then blinks quite quickly as her eyes begin to well up. I know what she is thinking but, God willing that is a long way off yet.

At some point in our walk we finally stumble upon the café, much to my relief and this is where I am treated to my annual ice cream. I know it is not good for me, but it just tastes so good! I can't think of a better way to start my tenth year than the way I spent it today with my People.

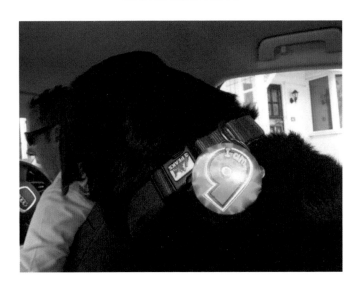

*Me with my birthday badge on our way to Crystal Palace Park!*

# THE FINAL CHAPTER

## *Double Figures: Infinity And Beyond*

Today is a very special day. Today is my 10th birthday – "Double figures!" Mummy declared as she wrapped her arms around my neck and snuggled her face deep into my fur. I raised my left paw up onto her shoulder to give the closest thing that I could to a hug. I always know when it is my birthday. There are presents wrapped in paper. Unlike cousin Thierry, I still have not learnt how to tear at the paper with my teeth to reveal the gift underneath. Somehow it seems a bit savage, a bit uncivilised and I prefer to have my People open them for me. Mummy always chooses suitably boyish paper for me.

It has been a strange and interesting life so far. I always think it odd that there are whole chunks of my life that my People know nothing about (unless of course they buy this and read it for themselves). Although Mummy has occasionally included me in her work life, there are large parts of her day that I know nothing about. Yet at the end of every day, we come back together, I wag my tail and attempt to lick her face. She tickles me behind the ears, and kisses me on top of my head and whatever stresses and strains we may have experienced (for her a feisty class of fifteen year olds, for me a feisty Alsatian or the knock of the postman at the door), they all seem to melt away.

Over the years Mummy and Daddy have noticed that I am increasingly reluctant to be away from home. I'm happy to go for my walks but I get anxious if I am away from home visiting relations, for example. They think it may be because I am scared of being left there. They think it goes back to the time when I was left in kennels when they went on holiday once. They may be right. I don't like to think of that awful time. It is true though that I do not let them out of my sight when we are visiting other people and by 5.30 p.m. I start to send them the signals that it's time to go. Mummy says I am becoming agoraphobic, whatever that means. Sounds quite intelligent!

In the five years since I have begun to write my memoirs, I have noticed some little changes. I now have a fair crop of little white hairs under my chin, although essentially my coat remains thick, lustrous and black and I am often mistaken by other Labrador owners for a much younger specimen.

I have a tendency to sleep for longer in the day and in fact throughout the evening too. No more do I snooze for ten minute snatches, nowadays my eyes roll right back into my head, my legs have been known to gallop in my sleep and my snoring often causes my People to turn up the volume on the TV. Most of the time they let me sleep, occasionally I am woken by the flash of a camera and recently footage of my slumbering was uploaded onto something called YouTube and got thousands of hits! Sounds painful!

Also, as I have already mentioned I now run out of puff when chasing the ball on the third or fourth occasion. The stiffness in my joints has eased up though as my People took me to the vet and got me some Glucosamine Chondroitin tablets to take each day and also bought me a paddling pool to splash around in although I mostly use it as a giant water bowl.

So maybe time is beginning to catch up on me physically, but mentally I am still a pup at heart. I still love to play chase in the garden with one of my many toys. I still love to lie on the sofa on my back with my legs in the hair having my People blow raspberries on my tummy.

In the time between snoozes, walkies and feeds I have tried to reflect upon what I have achieved so far and what I still wish to achieve in my twilight years. So in the thirty seconds of concentration I was able to devote to this I decided the following:

### Ten Brave Acts (Still to be achieved):

1.  Catching a burglar.

2.  Alerting the family to a fire in the house.

3.  Defending Mummy against a bad man.

4.  Chasing a cat out of the garden.

5.  Standing my ground against any of the Pembury Massive (or now I have moved, the Croydon Hardnuts.)

6.  Not jumping/cowering at a plastic bag, jogger, car unlocking, buses or any other innocuous sound.

7.  Not jumping when the fire in the fire place crackles and spits. (Now I have moved we do not have one of these, so that sorts that out nicely).

8.  Not panting and shaking at the sound of fireworks. This could be tricky as where we live now, they seem to have fireworks on any day with a 'Y' in it.

9.  Not to be scared of the rabbits. (Haven't seen too many of them where I have moved to).

10. Not being afraid of growing old.

Mummy says she is more than happy if I do not have to demonstrate my bravery with numbers 1 – 3 in particular, that number 4 is my key responsibility and that it would be useful if I could achieve numbers 5, 6, 7 and 8 and that she understands my fear of number 10. One she wishes to add is my being able to walk on floors that do not have a rug, runner or carpet on them – fat chance.

Benny, who is already quite old, says he is not worried anymore about being old. He says that when it is time to pass over we will cross a rainbow bridge and go to a better place that is continuous food and walkies. While that sounds lovely, I think I am very happy here, with my Mummy and Daddy. Although I am ten I still have plenty of get up and go (unlike Mummy who says hers 'Got up and Went'). And it's not a bad life. It's a very good one in fact. I have few regrets. Never seeing my Birth Mother again isn't one of them. My Mummy and Daddy have been everything a pup could want. For a dog's life, it hasn't been a bad life so far!

*This is my Buzz Lightyear 'To Infinity and Beyond!' pose. Others say it makes me look snooty. Not bad for a Fella from Essex.*

BYE BYE FOR NOW!

# A DOG'S LIFE

## *Epilogue*

Since writing the last chapter, sadly, my friend Benny passed away. Apparently, it was quick and he simply fell asleep and did not wake up again. He had his People with him and now lies buried under a tree in their garden.

Although I am sad I did not get to see Benny again, it's nice his leaving was so peaceful and that the people he loved were with him to the end. He would have been the first to declare what a good life he had and how loved he was. It is at this point, in my Senior Years that I am reminded of the words in that famous Bob Marley song:

"Don't worry about a thing. Cos every little thing's gonna be alright." Bob has become my hero as we discovered quite by accident one day when there was a thunderstorm that I quite liked Reggae music, but Bob Marley's songs in particular. As I listened to the music, I visibly calmed down and my breathing steadied. So now whenever it thunders or there are fireworks, my People get out his greatest hits and every little thing is alright.

*This is my message to you-hoo-hoo!*

11695706R00073

Printed in Great Britain
by Amazon.co.uk, Ltd.,
Marston Gate.